THE 14TH I

This book outlines the life of spiritual diplomacy of the 14th Dalai Lama and his emergence as a global peace icon. It traces his evolution as a Tibetan Buddhist monk rooted in the Geluk tradition, as a Nobel laureate, and as an internationally recognized peacemaker.

The volume brings to the fore the Dalai Lama's monastic life grounded in the compassion and ethical responsibility of a bodhisattva, somebody who is willing to renounce *samsara* for the benefit of others, as well as that of a political leader of Tibet. It examines the deep impact of his ideas of peacekeeping and universal responsibility on world politics, which draw on acceptance, inclusion, and respect as their central pillars. Further, this book highlights his departure from the practices of the earlier Dalai Lamas, and how the Chinese invasion and his exile in India transformed him into a universal figure of peace, rather than solely being the leader of Tibet.

An introspective read, this book will be of much interest to readers interested in spiritual diplomacy and political philosophy. It will also be of interest to scholars and researchers of peace and conflict studies, international relations, politics, and religion, especially Buddhism.

Mario I. Aguilar is Professor of Religion and Politics at the School of Divinity, St Mary's College, University of St Andrews, United Kingdom. A few of his recent publications include *Church, Liberation and World Religions: Towards a Christian–Buddhist*

Dialogue (2012), *Pope Francis: His Life and Thought* (2014), *Christian Ashrams, Hindu Caves, and Sacred Rivers: Christian–Hindu Monastic Dialogue in India 1950–1993* (2016), *The Way of the Hermit: Interfaith Encounters in Silence and Prayer* (2017), and *Interreligious Dialogue and the Partition of India: Hindus and Muslims in Dialogue about Violence and Forced Migration* (2018). His research interests include the study of religion; religion in the contemporary world; theology in Latin America and Africa; contextual theology; biblical studies and anthropology; Islam in Africa; the history of Tibet and Tibetan Buddhism; Christian–Buddhist dialogue; Hinduism, particularly monasticism in India; Christian–Hindu dialogue; and Hindu texts.

PEACEMAKERS

Series Editor: **Ramin Jahanbegloo,** *Executive Director of the Mahatma Gandhi Centre for Nonviolence and Peace Studies and the Vice-Dean of the School of Law at Jindal Global University, India*

Peace is one of the central concepts in the spiritual and political life of humanity. Peace does not imply the absence of war. It implies harmony, justice and empathy. Empathy is the key to education of peace in our world. In other words, despite the vast differences of values between cultures and traditions, it is still possible to grasp an understanding of one another, by 'empathy'. Throughout centuries, peacemakers have endorsed a 'shared human horizon', which according to them had the critical force of avoiding moral anarchy and relativism while acknowledging the plurality of modes of being human.

Today in a different manner and in a changed tone, but with the same moral courage and dissenting voice, this series on 'Peacemakers' offers the first comprehensive engagement with the problems of peace in our age, through a meticulous and thorough study of the lives and thoughts of peacemakers of all ages.

MAHATMA GANDHI: A NONVIOLENT PERSPECTIVE ON PEACE
Ramin Jahanbegloo

THE 14TH DALAI LAMA: PEACEKEEPING AND UNIVERSAL RESPONSIBILITY
Mario I. Aguilar

For more information about this series, please visit:
www.routledge.com/Peacemakers/book-series/PCMK

THE 14TH DALAI LAMA

Peacekeeping and Universal Responsibility

Mario I. Aguilar

Routledge
Taylor & Francis Group

LONDON AND NEW YORK

First published 2021
by Routledge
2 Park Square, Milton Park, Abingdon, Oxon OX14 4RN

and by Routledge
52 Vanderbilt Avenue, New York, NY 10017

Routledge is an imprint of the Taylor & Francis Group, an informa business

British Library Cataloguing-in-Publication Data
A catalogue record for this book is available from the British Library

Library of Congress Cataloging-in-Publication Data
A catalog record has been requested for this book

ISBN: 978-0-367-44254-5 (hbk)
ISBN: 978-0-367-44260-6 (pbk)
ISBN: 978-1-003-00859-0 (ebk)

Typeset in Sabon
by codeMantra

THIS WORK IS DEDICATED TO
TENZIN GYATSO, HIS HOLINESS
THE XIV DALAI LAMA
TO ALL TIBETANS

CONTENTS

SERIES EDITOR'S PREFACE

Peace is one of the central concepts of the spiritual and political life of humanity. When we study the world's religious and philosophical teachings, whether they are from the East or the West, we see that one of the basic ideals of all religions is peace. Peace does not imply simply absence of war. It implies harmony, justice, and empathy. Empathy is the key to education of peace in our world. In other words, despite the vast differences of values between cultures and traditions, it is still possible to grasp an understanding of one another, by "empathy." Therefore, we can maintain that all cultures have a shared core of common humanity. Throughout centuries, peacemakers endorsed a "shared human horizon," which according to them had the critical force of avoiding moral anarchy and relativism while acknowledging the plurality of modes of being human. As a matter of fact, the first step for peacemakers has always been to assume that not only there are differences among nations, cultures and traditions of thought, but also to admit that people may have different value systems, which need to be understood and approached dialogically and critically. Philosophy of peace is, thus, expressed here in the idea of a "self-respecting" community or nation, which strives to remove its own imperfections instead of necessarily judging others. As a result, peacemaking is always a call not only to cultivate humility but also to foster pluralism. Such a view is essential if we are to avoid the danger of cultural conformity and move towards the recognition of shared values of humanity and the acceptance of what Martin Luther King, Jr.

called the 'cosmic companionship'. Put differently, we can say that it would be an error to hope that we can ever achieve a truly universal vision of peace without an intercultural approach to the idea of civilization. Peacemakers have always been in favor of a farsighted peacemaking in our world, which has seriously advocated the logic of solidarity and civic friendship beyond national selfishness and global exclusion. Let us not forget that all peacemakers, either man or woman, young or old, from the West or the East, were all engaged in the process of peace seeking by fighting for care, openness, and empathy as constructive forms of being together. Today in a different manner and in a changed tone, but with the same moral courage and dissenting voice, this series on "Peacemakers" offers the first comprehensive engagement with the problems of peace in our age, through a meticulous and thorough study of the lives and thoughts of peacemakers of all ages.

Ramin Jahanbegloo

PREFACE

Every book starts as an open canvas in which colours are added until unsatisfied with the result. More so in the case of works about a religious leader and a globalised person, in this case my own portrait of the 14th Dalai Lama, the manifestation of Avalokiteshvara or Chenrezig, the Bodhisattva of Compassion and the Patron Saint of Tibet. Born in Tibet, he left his homeland for India in 1959 and has lived on exile in Dharamshala, northern India. However, the person of Dalai Lama in his Geluk robes has become part of the social imaginary in India and throughout the world. Millions have heard his message, and after receiving the Nobel Prize, many world leaders have honoured him with their hospitality and have sought his counsel. The message of the Buddha of Compassion and the exciting rituals, chanting and lives of Tibetans have permeated through Dalai Lama's encounter with humanity and he has made us better at being human and has reminded us of our material and spiritual nature. He has become one of the central peacemakers in the global scene, bringing people into a deep reflection about our shared humanity and our universal responsibility towards all humans, all sentient beings, and the cosmos.

I attended his teachings in Nottingham, London and Dharamshala, curious at first, enchanted later, and slowly becoming a scholar of Tibetan history and texts. As I outlined within this work, in order to understand the Dalai Lama, it is necessary to understand the developments of Tibetan Buddhism, and particularly the role and lineage of the Dalai Lamas. Within such history the oral transmission of texts becomes central to the passing of knowledge and the connections between the Tibetan Buddhist community and the leadership of the Dalai Lama. While I started my scholarly journey studying Tsongkhapa's *Lamrin Chenmo*, I have outlined within this work the centrality of the person of the Dalai Lama as a *bodhisattva*, and therefore I have outlined his teachings and commentaries on the *Bodhicharyāvatāra* (*The Way of the Bodhissattva*). His role as a peacemaker has been emphasised in each one of his visits and speeches throughout the world, and particularly in his engagement with Tibetan communities and Western communities of learning, particularly with the young in their search for meaning in life. This work outlines my own understanding of the Dalai Lama's role and life and I would hope that finds a resonance in what the 14th Dalai Lama would transmit about his life, his philosophy, and his people of Tibet.

Mario I. Aguilar
Nalanda Hermitage, May 2020

ACKNOWLEDGEMENTS

I acknowledge the teachings of the Dalai Lama on several occasions, and the moral support he has given over the years to the Centre for the Study of Religion and Politics (CSRP), which I direct at the University of St Andrews in Scotland. At the CSRP we researched over a period of ten years moments of Tibetan history, and I am very grateful to Geshe Lakhdor, director of the Library of Tibetan Works and Archives, for the opportunities he gave me to present my work to researchers and staff of such prestigious library during my stays in Dharamshala. I also acknowledge the support of the editorial staff of the journal *Tibet* for the publications that came out of such lectures. I am grateful to the Sikyong, Dr Lobsang Sangay, for his hospitality during a visit to Macleod Ganj (2014) and a long conversation on Tibetan politics and international affairs, together with a group of friends and former students. During the same visit I was introduced to Tibetan monastic life at the Geden Chöling (dga' ldan chos gling dgon pa) and I thank the nuns and their Abbott for making it possible for me to take part in some of their teachings. It is a fact that without the support and companionship of Glenda Tello none of this would have happened. I also acknowledge the ongoing encouragement of Gordon T. Barclay, and members of the Milarepa Foundation and the Laudato Si' International Group. Finally, my gratitude to Professor Ramin Jahanbegloo for inviting me to include my work in his series on "Peacemakers".

INTRODUCTION
The 14th Dalai Lama as peacekeeper

The 14th Dalai Lama (within this work 'the Dalai Lama') has been one of the most well-known religious figures for the past fifty years. His figure and his teachings of the Tibetan community throughout the world and particularly within Europe and the United States have influenced different generations of people but particularly the young. Thus, the Dalai Lama became a bridge between a secular West and a metaphysical East. As a result, Tibetan Buddhism has become part of Western practices and the Dalai Lama personally has influenced developments and changes within Buddhism, including the ordination of women monks.[1] However, within all those encounters and teachings the 14th Dalai Lama has emphasised his central persona as a simple monk and his identity as a Tibetan on exile in India since 1959. When asked, he has always defined himself as a simple Buddhist monk, an exile and a person of peace.[2] Indeed, the Dalai Lama's main role in the world, I would argue, has been that of a peacemaker, somebody who regards another person as an equal human being and therefore shares the same nature and activity within this world of materiality and *karma*. The Dalai Lama has joined a pantheon of peacemakers such as Mahatma Gandhi, Thomas Merton, Desmond Tutu, and Pope Francis who regardless of the challenges of life and the calls for war, death, and ethnic cleansing have maintained their position of acceptance, inclusion, and respect even towards those who occupied Tibet and triggered his exile in India. The Dalai Lama, together with Desmond Tutu, extended such art of peacemaking to its

1

fruit, joy, whereby those who have suffered exile and persecution are also those who treasure peace more than others. Together, they extended such enormous joy to the world.[3]

The Dalai Lama's resilience on issues of peace and a universal understanding has shown his closeness to India, the country of his exile, and the adherence to the Gandhian philosophy of *ahimsa*, a tradition of non-violence that the Dalai Lama praised when receiving the Nobel Prize in 1989.[4] The ancient Indian doctrine of *ahimsa* or non-violence, according to the Dalai Lama, 'has flourished and been adopted as a principle of peaceful coexistence by all faiths'; because *ahimsa* 'is not about physical non-violence. It also means non-violence in speech and thought'.[5] Thus, as a political leader and head of the Tibetan government on exile since 1959 until 2011 he could have pursued a direct philosophy of disdain and hatred towards the Han Chinese, and the government of China, towards those who in practice inflicted suffering and pain on Tibetans within China.[6] On the contrary, his message of compassion and peace towards China has been clear: 'we Tibetans harbor no hatred against our Chinese brothers and sisters, and [that] we Tibetans are neither anti-Chinese nor anti-China'.[7] Within his own community he has also been a peacemaker challenging younger militant Tibetans on their plausible violent approach of resistance to China not only by dismissing claims of Tibetan independence but also describing self-immolations as very sad. However, following the Dharma, the Dalai Lama looked at the intention behind self-immolations, arguing that 'those who sacrificed their lives with sincere motivation, for Buddha Dharma and for the well-being of the people, from the Buddhist or religious viewpoint, are positive'.[8] Nevertheless, if self-immolations were carried out with anger and hatred, according to the Dalai Lama, they could be considered wrong actions.

It is a fact that the development of a young Tibetan monk who arrived in India as a refugee and as a young political leader on exile took place over the years not only because of the experience of suffering by Tibetans but also as a result of many encounters with other political and religious leaders. However, the Dalai Lama learned also from the multiple encounters with thousands of individuals who left an impression on him and who asked him to be a peacemaker for the world. As a result of these encounters, the localised problems of Tibet became part of globalised questions by a shared humanity so that the Dalai Lama's sense that after all we are all human beings became a cry and a challenge for a universal responsibility towards peace, harmony, and the care of the environment for all sentient beings. The private self of a follower of the Buddha Dharma developed a public sphere of deep involvement and care indeed for all sentient beings. From a young age the Dalai Lama's teachers encouraged him to practice the six perceptions of the Mahayana path: generosity, morality, patience, perseverance, one pointed or meditative concentration, and penetrative insight into the inherently void nature of reality.[9] The principle of *karma's* understanding learned with wise teachers in Tibet became of central importance for his life as a *bodhisattva*, an enlightened being not because of a title but because of the love and altruism of renouncing his own self-path to reincarnation for the sake of others:

> Thus for everything that lives,
> As far as are the limits of the sky,
> May I be constantly their source of livelihood
> Until they pass beyond all sorrow.[10]

Therefore, the Dalai Lama's private self-identity also became a public path of aid to others whereby peace as a philosophical understanding became an altruistic way of life through peacekeeping. The Dalai Lama as a peacemaker became less concerned with the local affairs of his political realm but he became part of a self-declared global responsibility for all sentient beings, for the planet and for those in need of comfort. The Dalai Lama has spoken of the differences between the East and the West, terms that he has used, but at the same time he has emphasised that differences are 'minor' because we are all human beings, we have an equal right to be respected as human beings; in his words 'I want happiness but not suffering, just as you do'.[11] Further, for him human action must show a concern for others, and the feeling for the suffering of others as well as our own suffering, with a sense of universal responsibility.[12] However, within such dialogue with others the Dalai Lama has declared that he does not per se believe in the creation of institutions to foster such universal responsibility but that 'a genuine sense of responsibility can result only if we develop compassion'.[13] Such sense of universal responsibility connects with the Dalai Lama's disbelief in national boundaries because all human beings are the same.[14]

Indeed, one of the greatest gifts of Tibet to the world was to allow the West to encounter an ancient civilisation, the Buddha Dharma, its prayer flags, compassion, and gentleness within the West.[15] Such inter-connectedness between human beings was the first remark he made when he taught in the West for the first time Tsong-Kha-Pa's classical text *The Great Treatise on the Stages of the Path to Enlightenment*.[16] The text was so dear to him when he was still in Tibet that it was the only one that he brought out of Tibet when he fled to India in 1959. Thus, the Dalai Lama told his audience: 'In the first place, I am just one human being among six billion. The fact is that all six billion human beings share one planet. We all survive under one sun'.[17]

This work outlines critically the life of diplomacy and peace-making led by the 14th Dalai Lama arguing that his formation as a Tibetan Buddhist monk grounded in the Geluk tradition has made him into a person who can relate to others in peacefulness. His monastic life is fully grounded in the compassion and ethical responsibility of a *bodhisattva*, somebody who is willing to renounce exiting *samsara* for the benefit of others. As a Dalai Lama he has guided his people and many others into the appreciation of Tibetan Buddhism, and has aided with his teachings, fully grounded in Buddhism, to the realisation of peace between individuals and between communities. He has emphasised the unity and global responsibility of all human beings. His role as a peacemaker and a global leader for peace and responsibility has come from within so that in his own life, he has become a *bodhisattva*, more concerned with the welfare of others rather than his own. The contents of this work study the identity of the Dalai Lama as peacemaker through his personal development as a Dalai Lama (Chapter 1), as a *bodhisattva* (Chapter 2), as an exile and seeker of others (Chapter 3), as a teacher of global responsibility (Chapter 4), and as an advocate of non-violence and diplomacy (Chapter 5).

Notes

1 See for example Vicki Mackenzie, *The Revolutionary Life of Freda Bedi: British Feminist, Indian Nationalist, Buddhist Nun*. Boulder, CO: Shambala Publications, 2017.

2 'Biography of the Dalai Lama', in Subhash C. Kashyap (ed). *The Political Philosophy of the Dalai Lama: Selected Speeches and Writings*. New Delhi: Rupa Publications, 2014, pp. 573–582 at p. 582.

3 In April 2015 Desmond Tutu, also a Nobel Prize laureate, joined the Dalai Lama at his home in Dharamshala where they shared their stories, their religious practices, and ultimately their joy; see their conversations in The Dalai Lama and Desmond Tutu, *The Book of Joy*. London: Hutchinson, 2016.

4 The Dalai Lama, 'Tribute to Mahatma Gandhi: Nobel Prize Acceptance Speech, University of Aula, Oslo, 10 December 1989', in *The Political Philosophy of the Dalai Lama*, pp. 153–155.

5 '*Ahimsa* – India's Contribution to the Word: Talk to the UK Indian Communities', London, 20 September 2015, Program for the visit of His Holiness the Dalai Lama to the UK September 2015, p. 16.

6 The Dalai Lama has described his own experience of Chinese threats and provocations in Lhasa before 1959 and his journey into exile in his memoir *My Land and My People*. New York: McGraw-Hill, 1962.

7 The Dalai Lama, 'Message to the Chinese: Address to the Tibetan-Chinese Conference', Geneva, 6 August 2009, in *The Political Philosophy of the Dalai Lama*, pp. 355–358 at p. 355.

8 The Dalai Lama, 'Self-Immolations: Interview by NBC', 11 October 2012, in *The Political Philosophy of the Dalai Lama*, pp. 295–296 at p. 295.

9 A.A. Shiromany, 'Introduction', in A.A. Shiromany (ed). *The Spirit of Tibet: Vision for Human Liberation – Selected Speeches and Writings of H.H. The XIV Dalai Lama*. New Delhi: Tibetan Parliamentary and Policy Research Centre in association with Vikas Publishing House, 1996, pp. ix–xix at p. xv.

10 *Bodhicharyāvatāra* § 22. Throughout this work I use the translation of the *Bodhicharyāvatāra* from the Tibetan by the Padmakara Translation Group published as Shāntideva, *The Way of the Bodhisattva*. Boston, MA, and London: Shambala, 2006; see the Dalai Lama's commentary on the *Bodhicharyāvatāra* translated by the Padmakara Translation Group published as His Holiness the Dalai Lama, *For the Benefit of All Beings: A Commentary on the Way of the Bodhisattva*. Boston, MA, and London: Shambala, 2009, and its previous edition *A Flash of Lightning in the Dark of Night*. Boston, MA, and London: Shambala, 1994.

11 The Dalai Lama, 'Universal Responsibility and the Good Heart', in
    A.A. Shiromany (ed). *The Spirit of Tibet: Vision for Human Liber-
    ation*, pp. 118–139 at p. 118.
12 The Dalai Lama, 'Universal Responsibility and the Good Heart', in
    A.A. Shiromany (ed). *The Spirit of Tibet*, pp. 118–119.
13 The Dalai Lama, 'On Universal Responsibility', in A.A. Shiromany
    (ed). *The Spirit of Tibet*, pp. 140–156 at p. 143.
14 The Dalai Lama, 'On Humanity', Aurobindo Ashram, Auroville,
    24 December 1993, in A.A. Shiromany (ed). *The Spirit of Tibet*,
    pp. 157–165.
15 The theme of global responsibility can be particularly studied in the
    Dalai Lama's works *A Human Approach to World Peace*. Boston,
    MA: Wisdom Publications, 1984, and *Ethics for the New Millen-
    nium*. New York: Riverhead Books, 2001.
16 Tsong-Kha-Pa, *The Great Treatise in the Stages of the Path to En-
    lightenment*, 3 vols. Ithaca, NY: Snow Lion Publications, 2001,
    2002, and 2004.
17 The Dalai Lama, *From Here to Enlightenment: An Introduction
    to Tsong-Kha-Pa's Classic Text the Great Treatise on the Stages of
    the Path to Enlightenment*. Boston, MA, and London: Snow Lion,
    2012, p. 2.

1

BECOMING THE 14TH
DALAI LAMA

The 14th Dalai Lama was born on 6 July 1935 in a small farm-
ing family in Taktser, in the province of Amdo, northeast Tibet.[1]
The search for the incarnation of the 14th Dalai Lama had be-
gun in the summer of 1936, two and a half years after Thubten
Gyatso, known as the 13th Dalai Lama had died.[2] Following
custom, Retting Rinpoché, the Regent of Tibet, had convened
the Tibetan National Assembly in order to send out teams that
searched for the new Dalai Lama. Previously, the Regent and a
group of senior monks had visited the waters of Lake Lhamo
Latso and had a vision seeing three Tibetan alphabets (Ah, Ka,
Ma), a monastery with a three-tiered turquoise roof and a gilded
pagoda-like top, and a twisting tail leading east of the monastery to a bare hill and a small one-storey house with a blue roof.
For the Regent, the letter 'Ah' referred to Amdo and the search
party left for Amdo. After a couple of visits to his home by senior lamas, Tenzin Gyatso, was recognised as the incarnation
of the 13th Dalai Lama and he was enthroned in Potala on
22 February 1940.

The importance of the Dalai Lamas for Tibet cannot be down-
played and the formation and persona of the 14th Dalai Lama was
shaped by the Tibetan expectations of a religious Buddhist leader
who at the same time was expected to lead the politics of Tibet
as head of the Tibetan Government. It is clear from the conversations by Thomas Laird with the Dalai Lama that the Dalai Lama
assumed his full connection through the incarnational principle
with the thirteen previous Dalai Lamas.[3] Historically, the head

of the Geluk, a Tibetan monastic order (wearing yellow hats), became central to the history of Tibet because of the understanding and cooperation between the Third Dalai Lama and Altan Khan, a powerful prince of the Turmet Mongols who recaptured the ancient imperial Mongol capital of Karakorum ca. 1550. Khan invited the Third Dalai Lama to visit Mongolia in 1577.[4] The Third Dalai Lama travelled to Mongolia and in June 1578 they met exchanging titles and gifts. Altan Khan translated the common name of all Dalai Lamas 'Gyatso' as 'ocean' and keeping the name Lama, which has been traditionally applied to somebody recognised as a Tulku or to one's teacher gave the name 'Dalai Lama' to the head of the Buddhist masters of the Mongols.[5] Thus, the first and Second Dalai Lamas had not used such title and were given the title later, following the understanding that the title conferred by Khan to the Third Dalai Lama could and should be applied to the previous Dalai Lamas following laws of incarnation. The 14th Dalai Lama has played down any higher 'wisdom' attached to the name Gyatso as 'ocean', arguing that Gyatso is just a name.[6]

Regardless of titles it is clear that the visit of the Third Dalai Lama to the Mongols made an impact on Altan Khan and that all of them under his patronage converted to Buddhism, burned their traditional shamanic objects, and conferred noble titles to all Geluk monks who taught all the Mongols under Altan Khan.[7] The military protection of Altan Khan extended to Tibet and the following khans gave the same loyalty to their Buddhist teachers. While it is clear that with the aid of the khans the following Dalai Lamas made Tibet into a powerful nation vis-à-vis China, for the purposes of religious historiography and the Dalai Lama's heritage it is crucial to understand the historical and monastic life of the First, Second, and Third Dalai Lamas. Tibet through the nobility and the monasteries was already an organised feudal nation.

Dalai Lama I: Gendün Drup 1391–1474

The monk Gendün Drup [his birth name was Pema Dorje] was born in 1391 in a nomad family that lived near Sakya Monastery in Tsang.[8] On the evening after his birth bandits attacked the family and Gendün's mother hid him inside a cave where hagiographical writings tell us that he was protected from vultures by a single vulture. According to Shen Weirong 'this vulture was an embodiment of the Four-Faced Mahakala, which became the personal Yidan deity of Gendün Drup'.[9] After the death of his father at the age of seven he sought refuge with the community at Kadam Monastery in Tsang. He received the *genyen* (ordination) from Druppa Sherap the 14th abbot of Narthang and learned how to write and recite sacred texts. At the age of fifteen he was given his monastic name and ordained as a *getsul*. After five years he received the full ordination as a *gelong* at Narthang. Over the years he received instruction from more than sixty lamas throughout Tibet, most of them either Kadam or Geluk lamas. Thus, his unusual sense of monastic belonging and his wide education made him an example of religious diversity.

Together with another disciple of Tsong Khapa, a monk with the name of Sherap Sengee, Gendün Drup travelled extensively all over Tibet between the years 1426 and 1438, a reason for the consolidation of Tibetan Buddhism and the monasteries within Tibetan national life. It is possible to argue that he was a great monk given that he fulfilled the three areas required from those monks or lamas who were remembered through the ages in monasteries and through Tibetan life: (a) they were widely knowledgeable and scholarly oriented, (b) they were morally strict in following the three vows taken within Tibetan monastic life, and (c) they were generous in their availability to others. In the case of Gendün Drup, he fulfilled the first two conditions through his monastic life and his dedication to teaching. An example of his availability to others can be found, for example, in his rejection of his nomination as abbot of Ganden Monastery in Lhasa in 1450, a position that would have made him leader of the Geluk School. Instead, he decided to continue his journey from monastery to monastery, a practice that was going to be the exception to the rule with the increase of monastic communities and the absolute centrality of the Dalai Lama as a symbol of a unified Tibet.[10]

A prolific writer, his works were collected in six volumes among which there was an expertise in logic and extensive commentaries on Buddhist writings. Gendün Drup continued the practice of his master of celebrating the annual Mönlam Chemno festival and in 1474 he invited 1,600 monks to Tashilhünpo Monastery to celebrate a twelve-day festival that was attended by 10,000 monks. It was a clear sign that the Geluk school of Tibetan thought was clearly established within a variety of monastic traditions. He died in the same year and a year later a commemoration (Gong Dzok) was celebrated in his honour with more than two thousand monks taking part. His remains were kept until 1478 and then placed in a large *stūpa* made of silver and decorated with gold and copper.

Dalai Lama II: Gendün Gyatso 1475–1542

Gendün Gyatso wrote his autobiography in 1528 as well as his father's biography in 1509.[11] In his autobiography he described his birth as very auspicious of an important reincarnation and with the emphasis on his father's and mother's lineages already recognised as a lineage of important reincarnations within Tibetan Buddhism. I cite here from Amy Heller's translation:

> As soon as I was born, I looked about timidly and found beauty in front of me, and I smiled. My mouth was turned towards the direction of Tashilhünpo and my hands were in a gesture of devotion. My body was white like crystal, emanating a very pure light. My father immediately performed a special ritual for Cakrasamvara.[12]

By the time he was three years and annoyed with his mother, he threatened to leave for Tashilhünpo. Later, other signs such as the ease with which he composed sacred verses and his familiarity with monastic practices led the surrounding community realise that he was a reincarnation of Gendün Drup, who had had a spiritual home at Tashilhünpo Monastery. Nevertheless, his public recognition and enthronement took longer than usual because of the politics of that time. Some of the lamas, particularly the Abbott of Narthang, had animosities towards Gendün Gyatso's father and therefore they distrusted that the recognition of the reincarnation of an enlightened one could have come from such a father.[13] By the time that Gendün Gyatso was twenty years of age and a monk he suffered from the same controversies with other monks and one of the reasons why he didn't settle in one single monastery could have been because of the monastic politics of that time.

His main contribution to the development of the Geluk institutions was to expand their influence beyond Lhasa and Tashilhünpo. He served as abbot of three important monasteries in Central Tibet: Tashilhünpo (1512), Drepung (1517), and Sera (1528). He founded monasteries in the area East of Lhasa, particularly the important monastery of Chökhorgyal Metoktang in 1509. Located on the north banks of the Tsangpo this monastery became the home of the Dalai Lama's lineage and each Dalai Lama had to visit it once in their lifetime. In 1541 he founded the monastery of Ngari Dratsang to honour the relation of patronage with the kings of Guge in Central Tibet.

One of the central preoccupations of Gendüm Gyatso was politics of that time. In his writings he separated politics and the political into three different spheres: his engagement as a member of the lineage of the main teachers of Tibetan Buddhism, his engagement with the politics of his own monastic order, and the relationship with the Tibetan nobility through teaching that ultimately secured income for the monasteries and lands for further expansion.[14] During the period of Dalai Lama II there had been armed conflicts between the Karma and the Geluk Schools. The Karma members had already taken over Shigatse during the period of Gendün Drup and in 1480 they sent troops towards Ü in Central Tibet. By 1492 they occupied territories under control from Lhasa and in 1498 they occupied Lhasa itself. In 1517 and as Gendün Gyatso took over as abbot of Drepung the Geluk monks managed to drive the Karma Army away from Lhasa.

It was Gendün Gyatso who formalised the method to find a Geluk reincarnation. Monks went to a sacred lake called Lhamo Latso where the goddess Palden Lhamo lives in order to have visions about the location of the new incarnation of Chenziri, being the Tibetan name for the Bodhisattva (*bodhi* = enlightenment and *sattva* = being) *Avalokiteshvara* in Sanskrit. Thus, according to Thomas Laird,

11

Bodhisattvas are Buddhist saviours who work during the course of thousands of lifetimes for the benefit of others trapped in the prison of cyclic existence. They will not pass over into final enlightenment, and escape from the wheel of birth, death, and rebirth, until all other beings do so.[15]

Thus, the Bodhisattvas are altruistic beings who can visualise and feel the situation of others as their own and who identify themselves with the poor and the marginalised.[16] Gendün Gyatso expanded his influence through Central and Southern Tibet and prepared Tibetan Buddhism for its expansion into Mongol territory and the adoption of Tibetan Buddhism by the Mongols.

Dalai Lama III: Sönam Gyatso 1543–1588

The Third Dalai Lama was born at the beginning of the Tibetan year of 1543 in the state of Khangsargong in the region of Kyishö in Central Tibet.[17] His family had close ties with the Sakya School and with the political ruling group of Phakmo Drupa as his father was a district official and his mother's father, Wangchuk Rinpoché, was a well-known Tantric master serving the Tibetan royal household. His birth, as portrayed in most Tibetan biographies of somebody who has achieved full Buddhahood, was seen in dreams by her mother who had already experienced the death of several children at an early age. Therefore, the young boy was given milk from a white nanny goat and given the name Ranusi Chöpal Zangpo meaning 'the happy one protected by milk'.[18]

At the early age of two he showed signs of being the reincarnation of Gendün Gyatso and in 1546 the rulers of the House of Nedong recognised him and enthroned him in Drepung. When he took his first monastic vows, he was given the name Sönam Gyatso Pelzangpo Tanpe Nyima Chok Thamce Lenampar Gyalwa. In 1556, and after studying Mahāyāna Buddhist texts and being initiated into Tantric meditation cycles, he started travelling extensively, including his visits to monasteries located in Central Tibet such as Olkha, Chökhorgyal, Chonggyé, Tsethang, Nedong,

Samye, and Kyishö. Nevertheless, he developed a special bond with the community at Chökhorgyal Monastery, founded by the Second Dalai Lama and that became the home of the Dalai Lama lineage, monastery located close to the sacred 'lake of visions'.

Several invitations by the nobility were rejected by him; however, in 1558 he accepted an invitation by the ruler of Phakmo Drupa and he visited his residence at Nedong. A year later, Sönam Gyatso became the ruler's personal teacher until the ruler's death in 1564 while also becoming Abbott of Drepung in 1552 and Abbot of Sera in 1558. In 1554 he was ordained as a full monk. In 1568 he founded a personal temple, Dratshang Phende Lekshaling, today's known as the Namgyal Monastery that became incorporated as part of the West Wing of the Potala Palace in Lhasa by Dalai Lama V and became the Dalai Lama's private monastery.[19]

The Third Dalai Lama was an enthusiastic advocate of the Geluk School and taught the ways of the Geluk throughout Central Tibet. However, his main claim to fame was his teaching of Buddhism to the Mongols and the conversion of Altan Khan, the most important Mongol prince of that time, to Buddhism. In 1577 he rested in a small monastery that Rinchen Tsöndrü Gyaltsen, a hermit monk, had founded. He asked the hermit to build a larger monastery out of the small monastic foundation that in 1538 had been consecrated as Kumbum Jampaling. Kumbum became one of the most important Geluk monasteries and at the time of the 13th Dalai Lama had three thousand monks in its community.[20]

The beginning of the Dalai Lamas

It was in 1577 that the Third Dalai Lama received a second delegation from Altan Khan and started his journey to the Mongols, to the monastery of Thekchen Chökhorling where he arrived in 1578. Altan Khan and Sönam Gyatso entered into a relationship of a secular patron and a spiritual teacher whereby Altan Khan bestowed the Mongolian title of *ghaikhamsigh vcir-a dar-a say-in cogh-tu buyan-tu dalai*, translated by Karénina Kollmar-Paulenz as 'wonderful Vajradhara, good, brilliant, commendable ocean', 'dalai lama', or 'ocean lama'.[21] From that moment onwards the title was used for the previous incarnations of Sönam Gyatso and for every subsequent incarnation until the contemporary Dalai Lama, the 14th Dalai Lama. Sönam Gyatso also conferred a ritual title on Altan Khan, Chökyi Gyaplo Lhetshangpa Chenpo, which means 'Dharmarāja, Great Brahmā of the gods'.[22] Three months later the newly named Dalai Lama received an invitation to visit Beijing from the Ming emperor Wanli (1563–1620) but he did not accept the invite, returned to Tibet, and founded Chökhorling Monastery in Lithang in 1580.[23]

In 1582 Altan Khan died and his son Dügüreng Sengge invited the Third Dalai Lama to visit Mongolia. On his journey he founded Kumbum College and spent most of his remaining years in Mongolia. He died while teaching at Kharacin on the twenty-sixth day of the black month in the Year of the Earth Mouse of 1588. His remains were not transported back to Tibet and instead were deposited in a *stūpa* north of the Yeke-juu Temple in Kökekhota. The Third Dalai Lama only wrote one single volume with forty-two short entries; thus unlike his reincarnations who wrote abundantly he was 'a foremost missionary and traveller'.[24]

Dalai Lama IV: Yönten Gyatso 1589–1616

The Third Dalai Lama died in Mongolia at a moment when the Geluk had not secured their centrality in that country. It was there that the reincarnation of the Third Dalai Lama was recognised in the person of the son of a royal Mongolian family that could trace their lineage to that of Altan Khan. Thus, the Fourth Dalai Lama was the only one who was not a Tibetan; however, his finding in Mongolia rather than Tibet sealed a very close association between Tibet and Mongolia. Karénina Kollmar-Paulenz has suggested that 'if the Geluk wanted to consolidate their dominance among rival Tibetan Buddhist schools in Mongolia, they would need a charismatic person to succeed the 3rd Dalai Lama'.[25] The Geluk made a sharp political move by finding the Fourth Dalai Lama in Mongolia and as a result they secured their primacy in Tibet and Mongolia.

Yŏnten Gyatso, the Fourth Dalai Lama was born in January 1589, and his father was the eldest son of Dŭgŭreng Sengge, Altan Khan's own son. Thus, the position of the Fourth Dalai Lama was very powerful; he was the reincarnation of the Third Dalai Lama, but he was also a member of the royal Mongolian family and could exercise political power over Mongolia. However, a problem arose in Lhasa where the monks and nobility did not recognise the new Dalai Lama. A delegation of learned monks from Mongolia visited Lhasa in order to request the recognition of Yŏnten Gyatso as the Fourth Dalai Lama, but it took ten years for the actual official recognition to take place. A group of Tibetan lamas journeyed to Mongolia and subjected him to tests. After they were satisfied, they brought him back to Lhasa in 1602 where the new Dalai Lama was admitted into the first stages of the monastic community at the Jokhang.

The nobles of Tsang and other Buddhist orders challenged this newly acquired alliance between the Geluk and the Mongols. Thus, when the ruler of Tsang came to Lhasa for his initiation, he was refused entry into the Geluk order and was declared an enemy of the Geluk. The Fourth Dalai Lama immediately departed for Samye, a relatively secure place outside Lhasa. Eventually, Yŏnten Gyatso took full vows as a monk in 1614 at a time when the ruler of Tsang wanted to invade Central Tibet. The Mongols gathered their troops and prevented an attack by the feudal lords. The Fourth Dalai Lama died in the twelfth month in the Year of the Fire Dragon (1616) age twenty-seven. The causes of his death are not known and according to the Buddhist tradition a person who is enlightened exits human life as soon as he is ready. His ashes were placed in a *stūpa* near Drepung and he still remains as the only non-Tibetan Dalai Lama and the only one who did not occupy the see at Ganden.

Dalai Lama V: Ngawang Lopsang Gyatso 1617–1682

The Fifth Dalai Lama, known to Tibetans as 'the Great Fifth' managed to unify Tibet in 1642 at a moment when civil war was on the horizon. From the period of his enthronement in 1642 to the late 17th century the leadership of the Great Fifth managed to forge a Tibetan national identity centred upon the Dalai Lama, the Potala Palace, and the temples of Lhasa.[26] If previously the Dalai Lama was no more than another incarnation associated with a particular Buddhist school, the Fifth Dalai Lama became, due to his good works and influence, the protector of Tibet, a *bodhisattva*, a saintly figure of Mahāyāna Buddhism, who by his actions protected Tibet and in doing so served all humanity. By the time of his death the Fifth Dalai Lama had been given a status of *Bodhisattva Avalokiteśvara* and that of a Buddha, divine characteristics that were to be assumed as present in the lives of all the following Dalai Lamas. The political period of the Great Fifth has been assumed as an important political period in which, according to the Tibetan history by Shakabpa, despite its spiritual rule the Great Fifth became the de facto the ruler of Tibet 'despite the fact that the Qoshot Mongolian Gushri Khan and his heirs maintained the title of king of Tibet'.[27] On being the ruler of Tibet under the patronship of the Moguls the Great Fifth conducted the political affairs of Tibet without any involvement from China.[28]

The Fifth Dalai Lama was born into a noble family in Chingwar Taktsé Castle at Chonggyé, Yarlung Valley, near the tombs of the Tibetan kings in Chongye in the ninth month of 1617.[29] After being recognised because of his mother's dreams he was taken to Mongolia as to protect him from the infight between monks in Tibet and on his return he was sent to Drepung Monastery. At the monastery he learned how to read and already in 1623 he took part in a large feast for New Year being educated primarily by Lingmé Zhapdrug. In the same year he toured Central Tibet, a visit that was to take place every year since. In 1625 he met the First Panchen Lama, Lopsang Chökyi Gyaltsen (1570–1662) with whom he undertook studies of seminal Buddhist texts. In that year he also took vows as a novice monk before Panchen Rinpoché.

In 1637 the Great Fifth met with Gushri Khan, the Mongol leader, who was visiting monasteries in Central Tibet. After hearing the teachings of the Fifth Dalai Lama coinciding with auspicious dreams and an appearance of white light while travelling by night, Gushri Khan offered full protection to the Geluk. In return, the Fifth Dalai Lama conferred the title of 'Upholder of the Teaching, King of the Dharma' to Gushri Khan.[30] During that year the Dalai Lama received the vows of full ordination from Panchen Lozang Chökyi Gyeltsen before the image of Jowo Rinpoché. In 1638 Gushri Khan returned to Tibet with 300 people to whom the Dalai Lama gave teachings. In 1642 Gushri Khan asked the Fifth Dalai Lama to visit Tsang, a place that was already in the hands of the Mongols. It was in Shigatse that Gushri Khan offered the thirteen myriarchies of Tibet to the Fifth Dalai Lama. On that occasion, abbots of every Geluk, Kagyü, and Druk monasteries came to hear the teachings of the Fifth Dalai Lama who gave teachings on the Book of the Kadam.

In 1642 on the fifth day of the fourth month of the Water-Horse Year in the eleventh sexagenary cycle of the Tibetan calendar the Great Fifth was enthroned at the great audience hall of Samdruptsé Castle in Zhikatsé. He was raised on the high golden fearless snow lion throne and invested with the Tibetan leadership while Gushri Khan and Zhelngo Chöpel were seated on lower thrones.[31] This was a moment which I have termed 'the unification of Tibet' and in which the Geluk became recognised as primus inter pares by all other monastic orders simply because they brought unity and prosperity to Tibet through their alliance with the Mongols who became military protectors of Tibet.[32] The Geluk became spiritual protectors of the Mongols.

In 1645 Gushri Khan and the Fifth Dalai Lama looked for a place where they could build a fortress from where the leader of Tibet could lead all Tibetans. The Potala Palace was built over the years that followed and the Fifth Dalai Lama moved from Drepung to the Potala in Lhasa. The influence of the new Tibetan government grew due to the appointment of competent senior advisers, regents of the Tibetan government, who were in charge of administrative affairs and the whole of Tibet was unified under the centrality of one person: the Dalai Lama.

The rising importance of the Fifth Dalai Lama triggered an invitation from the Chinese Emperor Shunzhi (1638–1661) for the Dalai Lama to visit China. The Fifth Dalai Lama journeyed to China in 1652 and arrived in China the following year. Lhasa started being a place where foreigners arrived and visited. During the late part of the 17th century Armenians established a trading post, Mongols visited Lhasa in connection to diplomatic missions, new artisans were employed as painters, sculptors, and builders, while Indians also visited the newly erected fortification at Lhasa.[33]

The Fifth Dalai Lama managed to alter the hierarchical positions of the Tibetan monasteries by arranging sittings at the Mönlam Chenmo Festival, an annual festival instituted by Tsong Khapa in 1409. The new sitting order placed monks from the Dalai Lama's monastery of Drepung at the top of the hierarchy while making monks of Sera Monastery secondary to the proceedings.[34] A prolific writer, the Fifth Dalai Lama produced a substantial body of 25 volumes on different aspects of Buddhism that together with the corpus produced by his regent aimed at unifying religious thought and political practice in Tibet. In 1679 the Fifth Dalai Lama abdicated and left political powers to Sanggye Gyatso, dying three years later, on 7 April 1682. His death was not disclosed until April 1695 and his mummified body taken out of its mortuary casket. In November 1695, the public announcement of his death was finally made coinciding with the announcement of his reincarnation in the Sixth Dalai Lama and the enthronement of the new spiritual leader of Tibet on 8 December of the same year. The monasteries grew and the nobility of Tibet managed a feudal state throughout the reign of the following Dalai Lamas, until the ascent to the throne of Lhasa by the 13th Dalai Lama who started some of the reforms that influenced the life and socio-religious expectations put on the 14th Dalai Lama.

Notes

1 See the latest biographical summary as 'Biography of the Dalai Lama', in Subhash C. Kashyap (ed). *The Political Philosophy of the Dalai Lama: Selected Speeches and Writings*. New Delhi: Rupa Publications, 2014, pp. 573–582.
2 'Biography of the Dalai Lama', in *The Political Philosophy of the Dalai Lama*', p. 573.
3 Thomas Laird, *The Story of Tibet: Conversations with the Dalai Lama*. London: Atlantic Books, 2007, chapter 7.

4 Laird, *The Story of Tibet*, p. 142.
5 Laird, *The Story of Tibet*, p. 142.
6 Laird, *The Story of Tibet*, p. 143.
7 Laird, *The Story of Tibet*, p. 143.
8 See Glenn H. Mullin, 'Kun-ga Gyal-Tsen's' Life of the Dalai Lama I: The Twelve Wondrous Deeds of Omniscient Gen-Dun Drub', *The Tibet Journal* 10, 1985/4, pp. 3–42, and *The Fourteen Dalai Lamas: A Sacred Legacy of Reincarnation*. Santa Fe, NM: Clear Light Publishers, 2001; and Shen Weirong, 'The First Dalai Lama Gendün Drup 1391–1474', in Martin Brauen (ed). *The Dalai Lamas: A Visual History*, pp. 33–41, Chicago, IL: Serindia Publications, 2005.
9 Shen Weirong, 'The First Dalai Lama Gendün Drup 1391–1474', in Martin Brauen (ed). *The Dalai Lamas: A Visual History*, p. 33.
10 Shen Weirong, 'The First Dalai Lama Gendün Drup 1391–1474', in Martin Brauen (ed). *The Dalai Lamas: A Visual History*, pp. 34, 37.
11 For II Dalai Lama I follow the work by Amy Heller, who translated the autobiography of Gendün Gyatso for her doctoral thesis in 1992 and who wrote 'The Second Dalai Lama Gendün Gyatso 1475–1542', in Martin Brauen (ed). *The Dalai Lamas: A Visual History*, pp. 43–50; see also Glenn H. Mullin, 'De-Si Sang Gye Gya-Tso's: The Life of the Second Dalai Lama', *The Tibet Journal* 11, 1986/3, pp. 3–16, and *The Fourteen Dalai Lamas: A Sacred Legacy of Reincarnation*. Santa Fe, NM: Clear Light Publishers, 2001.
12 Amy Heller, 'The Second Dalai Lama Gendün Gyatso 1475–1542', in Martin Brauen (ed). *The Dalai Lamas: A Visual History*, p. 44, Chicago, IL: Serinidia Publications, 2005.
13 Heller, 'The Second Dalai Lama Gendün Gyatso 1475–1542', in Martin Brauen (ed). *The Dalai Lamas: A Visual History*, p. 50.
14 Heller, 'The Second Dalai Lama Gendün Gyatso 1475–1542', in Martin Brauen (ed). *The Dalai Lamas: A Visual History*, p. 43.
15 See Thomas Laird, *The Story of Tibet*, p. 12.
16 Nirmal Chandra Sinha, *Prolegomena to Lamaist Polity*. Calcutta: Firma K.L. Mukhopadhyay, 1969, p. 35.
17 For outline of biographies of the Third Dalai Lama see Karénina Kollmar-Paulenz, 'The Third Dalai Lama Sönam Gyatso and the Fourth Dalai Lama Yönten Gyatso', in Martin Brauen (ed). *The Dalai Lamas: A Visual History*, pp. 53–61, Chicago, IL: Serinidia Publications. The main biography of III Dalai Lama was written by the Fifth Dalai Lama who compiled shorter hagiographical works available during his lifetime; see also the important works by Glenn H. Mullin, 'Tse-Chok-Ling's Biography of the Third Dalai Lama', *The Tibet Journal* 11, 1986/3, pp. 23–39 and *The Fourteen Dalai Lamas: A Sacred Legacy of Reincarnation*. Santa Fe, NM: Clear Light Publishers, 2000.

18 Karénina Kollmar-Paulenz, 'The Third Dalai Lama Sönam Gyatso and the Fourth Dalai Lama Yönten Gyatso', in Martin Brauen (ed). *The Dalai Lamas: A Visual History*, p. 53.
19 Karénina Kollmar-Paulenz, 'The Third Dalai Lama Sönam Gyatso and the Fourth Dalai Lama Yönten Gyatso', in Martin Brauen (ed). *The Dalai Lamas: A Visual History*, p. 54.
20 Wilhelm Filchner, *Om mani padme hum: meine China – und Tibetexpedition 1925/28*, Leipzig: F.A. Brockhaus, 1929.
21 Karénina Kollmar-Paulenz, 'The Third Dalai Lama Sönam Gyatso and the Fourth Dalai Lama Yönten Gyatso', in Martin Brauen (ed). *The Dalai Lamas: A Visual History*, p. 58.
22 Karénina Kollmar-Paulenz, 'The Third Dalai Lama Sönam Gyatso and the Fourth Dalai Lama Yönten Gyatso', in Martin Brauen (ed). *The Dalai Lamas: A Visual History*, p. 58.
23 Karénina Kollmar-Paulenz, 'The Third Dalai Lama Sönam Gyatso and the Fourth Dalai Lama Yönten Gyatso', in Martin Brauen (ed). *The Dalai Lamas: A Visual History*, p. 59.
24 Karénina Kollmar-Paulenz, 'The Third Dalai Lama Sönam Gyatso and the Fourth Dalai Lama Yönten Gyatso', in Martin Brauen (ed). *The Dalai Lamas: A Visual History*, p. 59.
25 Karénina Kollmar-Paulenz, 'The Third Dalai Lama Sönam Gyatso and the Fourth Dalai Lama Yönten Gyatso', in Martin Brauen (ed). *The Dalai Lamas: A Visual History*, p. 60.
26 For an extended biography of the Fifth Dalai Lama, see Kurtis R. Schaeffer, 'The Fifth Dalai Lama Ngawang Lopsang Gyatso', in Martin Brauen (ed). *The Dalai Lamas: A Visual History*, pp. 65–91.
27 'Translator's Introduction to "Chapter 7: Great Fifth Dalai Lama assumes Political Power over Tibet"', in Tsepon Wangchuk Deden Shakabpa (ed). *One Hundred Thousand Moons: An Advanced Political History of Tibet*, vol. I. Leiden and Boston, MA: Brill, 2010, pp. 321–325 at p. 321.
28 'Translator's Introduction to "Chapter 7: Great Fifth Dalai Lama Assumes Political Power over Tibet"', in Tsepon Wangchuk Deden Shakabpa (ed). *One Hundred Thousand Moons*, vol. I, p. 323.
29 Tsepon Wangchuk Deden Shakabpa, *One Hundred Thousand Moons*, vol. I, p. 327.
30 Kurtis R. Schaeffer, 'The Fifth Dalai Lama Ngawang Lopsang Gyatso', in Martin Brauen (ed). *The Dalai Lamas: A Visual History*, p. 68.
31 Tsepon Wangchuk Deden Shakabpa, *One Hundred Thousand Moons*, vol. I, p. 347.
32 Mario I. Aguilar, 'Ngawang Lopsang Gyatso, *chösi nyitrel*, and the Unification of Tibet in 1642', *The Tibet Journal* XLI/2, 2016, pp. 3–20.

33 Kurtis R. Schaeffer, 'The Fifth Dalai Lama Ngawang Lopsang Gyatso', in Martin Brauen (ed). *The Dalai Lamas: A Visual History*, p. 70.
34 See *Guidelines for Seating Arrangements at the Mönlam Chenmo Festival of Lhasa* (1675) cited in Kurtis R. Schaeffer, 'The Fifth Dalai Lama Ngawang Lopsang Gyatso', in Martin Brauen (ed). *The Dalai Lamas: A Visual History*, pp. 70, 74; and Mario I. Aguilar, 'Densa Sum, Sendregasum, and the Three Seats: The Role of Gelugpa Monasteries in Tibet (1409–1959)', *The Tibet Journal* XL/1, 2015, pp. 23–40.

2

THE BODHISATTVA AS PEACEKEEPER

The spiritual and political formation of the 14th Dalai Lama, required a full engagement with the traditions of Buddhism, memorizing the great Indian Buddhist classics in Tibetan, studying them using logic, and debating them guided by his tutors.[1] Later, he read hundreds of commentaries on those texts in order to develop a debating style with which to pass the examination for his Geshe degree (doctorate in Buddhist studies).[2] He was also instructed on the ongoing socio-political problems of Tibet by his teachers, especially the Regent. Before his life in exile the Dalai Lama was expected to lead a government that provided support for its population, most of them monks, and that at the highest level of political tension had to deal with the nobility's clashes for access to the Tibetan government as well as disputes regarding lands, marriages, and the role and centrality of the monasteries. Further, the upkeep of monasteries and the formation of educated lamas required a constant guidance by the Dalai Lama as head of the Geluk Tibetan monastic order (the yellow hats), while other senior monks had slightly different ideas about their traditions and the running of their own monasteries.[3] Thus, the Dalai Lama had to be fully educated in many areas of Tibetan philosophy, science, religion, and politics, in order to manage a creative and peaceful tension between the different groups of monks, Tibetan civil servants, and nobles in Tibet.[4]

Among the very difficult subjects learned by all Dalai Lamas were the writings of Tsongkhapa, founder of the Geluk, and the traditions of other spiritual masters. The Dalai Lama intimated to Thomas Laird that he has dreamt of Tsongkhapa and that he enjoyed studying his commentaries and his connections to Atisha, the Indian reformer of the 11th century.[5] However, his life on exile in India brought new challenges to the continuity of the office of the Dalai Lama as he was expected to guide Tibetans in their challenging adaptation to life in India, Europe, and North America. By the time that the Dalai Lama sought protection in India very little was known about Tibet in India or Europe and the Tibetan tradition of Buddhism known as Lamaism was distrusted by many because of its mixture of traditional Bon religion and developments of Buddhism in Tibet after its arrival through the Indian masters. After 1959 Tibetan Buddhism became known to Western audiences, having been brought outside India and Tibet by monks that were fostered in their formation by Freda Bedi in Delhi, the first nun to be ordained in the Tibetan tradition, under the auspices of the Karmapa.[6]

The recognition of the Dalai Lama's contribution to the contemporary world by the conferral of the Nobel Prize for Peace in 1989 led to a new relationship between the Dalai Lama and the Western world. By conferring the Nobel Prize to the Dalai Lama, the Nobel Committee recognized that 'he based his Buddhist peace philosophy on reverence for all living things and the idea of universal responsibility that embraces both man and nature'.[7] The Nobel Committee recognized that his contribution to peace was significant because he didn't take a violent path as a result of the violence by China on the Tibetan people.[8] As a result, and after 1989, the Western world focused more and more on the contribution by the Dalai Lama to a universal responsibility for peace and as a result international groups of Buddhists requested him to teach important Tibetan texts that provided the international foundation for such universal responsibility and that made the Dalai Lama to be recognized as a peacekeeper.

The Dalai Lama has taught several of those texts to monks, those searching for enlightenment, and particularly groups of young people interested in Tibetan Buddhism. His own choice of texts has been grounded on texts that made Tibetan Buddhism distinct from other branches of Buddhism. Thus, through meditation techniques in order to achieve enlightenment and an ongoing effort to bring the end of suffering to all rather than a few, the foundational characteristic of Tibetan Buddhism became known as distinctive through public talks and engagement with the public by the 14th Dalai Lama. However, those contemporary choices arose out of his own choice made when on a cold night of March 1959, the Dalai Lama left Lhasa to seek exile in India. He could carry with him very few precious objects, as he was disguised as an ordinary soldier going through the crowds that had gathered in Lhasa. He carried his own copy of Tsongkhapa's *lam rim chen mo* – the *Great Treatise on the Stages of the Path to Enlightenment*.[9] Tsongkhapa wrote the *Great Treatise* in 1402, in the fourth year after his complete enlightenment, in the Yama-tongue Cave on the Oeudey Gungyal Mountain above the hermitage at Olkha where he had spent his five-year-long retreat. His intention was to bring Buddhism to others and to provide such path to enlightenment to as many human beings as possible. The text of the *Great Treatise* was translated into English for the first time by the students of the Venerable Geshe Wangyal who established a monastery in Washington, New Jersey, in 1958 and who throughout the 1960s and 1970s taught at Columbia University.[10] In 2008 the Dalai Lama taught this text at Lehigh University outlining his three main life commitments: as a human being the essential values of intelligence and compassion, as a Buddhist monk who embraces within the principles of the four-square path of the great religion traditions outside Buddhism (i.e. Judaism, Christianity, and Islam, and the spiritual traditions of secular humanism), and as a Tibetan seeking peaceful reconciliation with all people, particularly with the Chinese who could count as Tibet's worst enemy.[11]

Among those texts learned and taught by the Dalai Lama, Shantideva's *Bodhicharyāvatāra* has become central for his engagement with the contemporary world.[12] As outlined within the previous chapter when the Dalai Lama was found and brought to Lhasa his education was certainly that of religious and political leader for his own Tibetan people. Later, and in exile he continued being such leader and a Tibetan monk. Nevertheless, one could argue that after he received the Nobel Prize he was forced to engage with the contemporary world outside his Tibetan community by the many invitations that he received and since the 1990s by the need to seek support for Tibet as China became stronger about her claims on Tibet and the Dalai Lama's threat to Chinese unity. Thus, the Dalai Lama's speeches to supporters of Tibet were enriched by his contribution to ways and means of achieving world peace, particularly in his meetings with world leaders and his recognition as a peacekeeper by the United States. It is my argument within this chapter that the Dalai Lama's firm grounding on Shantideva's *Bodhicharyāvatāra* made him a peacekeeper in motion that ceaselessly addressed the problems of world peace by first responding to the need of everyone to be at peace. The monk that meditated every morning and who studied texts was a peacekeeper not only because of his ideas about peace but because he was first and foremost a monk that was at peace with himself. The translator of the Dalai Lama's continuous teaching of Shantideva's text recognized how unusual was for the Dalai Lama to teach in Tibetan a single text to a public audience in the Dordogne, France, in August 1991.[13] The whole teaching cycle marked a moment in which Tibetan texts were being offered to the contemporary world as universal works for world peace. Issues of universal responsibility became the universal teaching of a peacekeeper so that in the Dalai Lama's understanding 'Outer disarmament comes from inner disarmament. The only true guarantee of peace lies within ourselves'.[14]

Buddhist identity and a shared humanity

The Dalai Lama received the transmission of the *Bodhicharyā-vatāra* from Tenzin Gyaltsen, the Kunu Rinpoché who had received it from a disciple of Dza Patrul Rinpoché. However, his identity as a Tibetan from his parents framed his awareness of having been discovered as the new Dalai Lama due to a Tibetan identity in which the laws of *karma* are central to any social understanding. Brought up in Tibet under the daily practices of a family that made offerings, aided the poor, revered their lamas, and worked hard under the harsh conditions of the Himalayan snow, his identity was completely shaped by surroundings in which prayer wheels and prayer flags spoke of sharing with others. Indeed, the *Bodhicharyāvatāra* outlined instructions by Shantideva to acquire a path that can finally remove suffering by understanding the Four Noble Truths but in the Tibetan sense aid other sentient beings to do the same. A communal identity of a shared humanity arises out of a text that reflects the developments of Tibetan Buddhism not as an individual philosophy but as a socio-communal way of life in which the acquiring of *bodhicitta* aims at the formation of a *bodhisattva* who instead of leaving the cycle of suffering remains within such cycle in order to aid others in need. Identity then becomes not an individual trace but a communal one dictating laws of human interaction, nature, and metaphysics that provide for the relatedness of human beings and sentient beings. Identity then depends on a shared humanity while a shared humanity depends on a *bodhisattva*. The text of the *Bodhicharyāvatāra* remains central to Tibetan identity as the possibility of attaining Buddhahood despite one's impediments by attachment and greed, and it has remained central to the life of the Dalai Lama and his own understanding that since Tibet embraced Buddhism 'we have been wedded to the doctrine of peace and goodwill'.[15]

Shantideva's sense of teaching made into a text was directly linked with his sense of negative emotions and he self-reflected on the path required to overcome them.[16] Indeed, the Dalai Lama's teachings on his own life as a *bodhisattva* are outlined within his *Commentary* on the *Bodhicharyāvatāra*. In his *Commentary* he argues that the teachings of the Buddha can be divided into those that relate to *activity*, understood as refraining from harming others, and of a central *view* that refers once and again to the principle of interdependence.[17] This interdependence has its foundations on the acceptance that happiness and suffering and the beings who experience them do not arise without cause or are generated by a creator being. Thus, 'all things arise from causes corresponding to them'.[18] Interdependence shows us that single causes for happiness or affliction do not exist but that multiple and complex causes are interconnected.[19] Thus, the training of the mind as to see reality through interdependence 'makes our minds more relaxed and open'.[20] The view of interdependence can guide our actions because all actions are what Buddhism calls *karma*, the law of cause and effect, whereby the actions of the past have an impact on today, and our actions of today condition our attitudes in a future life.[21]

Given the Dalai Lama's identity as a *bodhisattva*, the self-identity of a *bodhisattva* becomes central to understand the decision making of a Tibetan head of state in exile who has guided his own Tibetan people towards a peaceful response at all times. He has had to crush some younger Tibetans who have advocated an armed response to the Chinese presence and violation of human rights in Tibet and particularly in Lhasa, the Tibetan capital. For his *Commentary* on Shantideva's teachings, and indeed on Buddhism, makes clear that 'an action is called negative or evil if it results in suffering' and 'it is called positive or virtuous if it results in happiness'.[22] The subduing of one's mind becomes then the tool for motivation so that 'a mind that is under control will be happy and at peace'.[23] The antidote to hatred, for example of the Chinese because of their wrong deeds against the Tibetans, is love, so that training the mind gives the possibility of transforming the way one acts, speaks, and thinks.[24] But the Dalai Lama's teachings are of course centred completely on the teachings of the Buddha and within this work it is important to appreciate the continuity and transmission of Buddhist teachings. Thus, the 14th Dalai Lama can be appreciated as his own person, but he cannot be understood without following the centrality of transmission within Buddhism, including the laws of reincarnation in the so-called Dalai Lamas. Individuality and interdependence go together, and the right intention through the training of the mind changes a selfish person into a person who is always looking at what is best for an interconnected world of sentient beings.

A Buddhist identity assumes a different epistemology than those of the Greeks and Romans and the perception of diversity in unity rather than universalism in commonality becomes central to the development of a self-identity. The training of the mind and meditation shape human epistemology rather than the unification of the senses through study. The basic teachings of the Buddha provide the foundation for such path toward the end of the suffering within the Mahāyāna tradition. For, in Buddhist historiography, after attaining -enlightenment, the Lord Buddha turned the Wheel of *dharma* setting his teachings in three stages.[25] The Buddha taught the Four Noble Truths, the basis of all Buddhism; then he taught the teachings on emptiness and the detailed aspects of such path; and third, he taught the teachings of emptiness in a more accessible fashion.[26]

The text of the *Way of the Bodhisattva* can be divided for the sake of reading and understanding in three sections: I–III 'The Excellence of *Bodhichitta*', 'Confession', and 'Taking Hold of *Bodhichitta*' are by nature devotional, intended to stimulate the appearance of *bodhichitta* in the mind; IV–VI 'Carefulness', 'Vigilant Introspection', and 'Patience' instruct on how to avoid the dissolution of *bodhichitta*; and VII–IX 'Diligence', 'Meditative Concentration', and 'Wisdom' suggest ways in which *bodhichitta* could be intensified.[27]

If one examines chapters 3 and 6 of the *Bodhicharyāvatāra* one can grasp the depth of compassion and wisdom that is required of a *bodhisattva* and that was taught to the Dalai Lama by his teachers and Buddhist masters. For in every Tibetan Buddhist text praise is first given to those who acquired a state of compassion and who attained the end of their suffering in previous times and previous lives. Thus, chapter 3 of the *Bodhicharyāvatāra* becomes a clear teaching of the descriptive self-identity of those who want to acquire *bodhichitta*. For intention rules the first movement towards an end of ignorance that masters suffering and therefore 'relieves all beings from the sorrows of the states of loss'.[28] Loss refers to a state in which negativity abounds and therefore the positive energy to bring beings in the lower realms is not sufficient as to bring them to higher realms.[29] Those at loss in a very graphic Tibetan historiography and imagery-painting on *thangkas*, walls, and paintings are referred by the *dharma* as animals, hungry ghosts, and beings in the hells.[30] The uneducated reader would comment that even the black imagery of hungry ghosts would alert those who have not studied texts on the dangers of negativity, and indeed those powerful images were the teaching tools for Tibetans who didn't know how to read or didn't have access to a teacher or indeed Tibetan books. They were most probably most of the population including monks that relied on the oral teaching at the general level when they entered the monasteries. They followed the instructions in the text and followed Shantideva who spoke thus 'so I join my hands and pray the Buddhas who reside in every quarter' with the intention of a *Bodhisattva* so that the Buddhas would kindle the *dharma's* light 'for those who grope, bewildered, in the dark of pain'.[31]

Chapter 3 expands in an overarching manner the plausibility of acquiring *bodhichitta* by the ongoing rejection of negativity that would lead not only to guide others in the *dharma* but to support others in their journey out of suffering without oneself being willing to exit the human cycle in order to continue guiding others. For the wish is for those enlightened beings to be among us.[32] Merit then is achieved by the seven branch prayer: homage, offering, confession, rejoicing in all good actions, the request for teaching, the request that the teachers remain in the world and not pass into *nirvana*, and dedication.[33] But once actions are desired for others, all those actions can be directed at others so that their pain may end, and be destroyed.[34] Chapter 3.8 remains a central paradigm of Tibetan Buddhism and has been recited at many gatherings and even at academic lectures and becomes a central portfolio of the possibility of compassion rather than a self-centred preoccupation for my own achievement of *nirvana*: 'may I become for them, the doctor, nurse, the medicine itself.[35] Thus, the *Bodhisattva* appears to alleviate suffering understood as negativity and ignorance and as a result to alleviate thirst and famine in the aeons, an intervallic aeon, an age of extreme instability and famine, the *antarakalpa*, an age of decline in the ancient Indian conception of four temporal sequences (*kalpa*), according to the *Dharmasangraha*, section 87.[36]

The cosmological intention, as authority and responsibility, refers to all sentient beings so that the priority of the poor and destitute requires the *Bodhisattva* to become 'a treasure ever-plentiful'.[37] Such relation of availability and closeness allows for the plausibility of helping sentient beings in their needs.[38] Body, possessions, and merits can be transferred to sentient beings in order to benefit sentient beings, including merits still to be gained.[39] Moreover, *nirvana* is attained by giving all so that the striving of one's life becomes compassion towards others, one's surrounding in a moment because 'it is best to give it all to others'.[40] The giving of one's body to others, for their intentions and wishes is not part of one's worries, even when 'they treat it like a toy, or make of it the butt of every mockery'.[41] The reader would begin to understand the connections between Tibetan attitudes towards the plausible annihilation of the body through ascesis, and the lack of concern, in a Western sense, for the admiration of bodies as part of a human social phenomenon. Indeed, the ongoing compassion of the Dalai Lama to the Chinese and their ongoing detentions of Tibetan monks, their torture, and the immolations of the past ten years connect directly to Shantideva's teachings: 'Whenever they may think of me, let this not fail to bring them benefit'.[42] In Tibetan terms, they wish following Shantideva the fortune of enlightenment to 'all those who slight me to the face or do to me some other evil'.[43]

The text returns to those who are lost in negativity and ignorance and asks of the *Bodhisattva* to be a guard for those without protection, a guide for them on the journey from ignorance to enlightenment, and for those who want to cross waters 'may I be a boat, a raft, a bridge'.[44] Further, the *Bodhisattva* wishes to be an isle in the midst of water, a lamp for those needing light, a bed for those needing rest, and a slave for those needing a servant.[45] However, within those material metaphors the text recognizes that to abide with the *dharma*, to train the awakened mind, and the training of oneself are all done 'for the benefit of beings'.[46]

Peacekeeping in the different textual commentaries

The Way of the Bodhisattva as a text written in the 8th century C.E. precedes the Tibetan translation of the 9th century and through the centuries was commented upon in different manners by the different Tibetan monastic traditions. For any translation of the *Bodhicharyāvatāra* was a commentary, adjusted to different emphases according to the monastic identity of the author and the audience to which it was intended. The beauty of its poetry made it into a favourite among the Indian Buddhist texts, and Thupten Jinpa thus recalled:

> Like many young Tibetan monks, I had the privilege of memorizing the text in my early teens and thus had the honour to recite the entire work from heart many times, often in the comparatively cool nights of southern India where my monastery was based.[47]

The same act of memorization and therefore of actualization would have been expected from the Dalai Lama at a time when his monastic ideals would have mingled with those of the *bodhisattva* compassion as aid to others portrayed in chapter 3 of the *Bodhicharyāvatāra*.

The more mature Dalai Lama was able to appreciate the call to wisdom inherent in the text and that is present specifically in chapter 9.[48] Further, within his own commentary the Dalai Lama does not refer only to the work by Tsongkhapa, the founder of his own monastic order, but he relies significantly and in a peacekeeping role on masters from other traditions.[49] Thus, the Dalai Lama in his teachings over a weekend at Vajra Yogini Institute in Lavaur, France, in 1993, relied upon two 19th-century Tibetan commentators from different traditions reflecting not only their non-sectarian stand but the Dalai Lama's strong stand on non-sectarianism and his sense of peacekeeping between the different schools of Tibetan Buddhism.[50] Such non-sectarian start in Tibet was marked by the publication of an exposition of chapter 9 of *Bodhicharyāvatāra* by the Nyingma master Ju Mipham Namgyal Gyatso who was criticized, among others, by the Geluk author Drakkar Lobsang Palden.[51] Thus, the Dalai Lama used in his own teachings the work by Khenpo Künpal with Nyingma terminology as the Old translation school, and the work by Minyak Künso using the Geluk terminology, stressing the non-sectarian nature of the *dharma*.[52] Therefore, he also emphasized in the teaching of the *Bodhicharyāvatāra* the non-sectarian characteristics of Buddhism, after years as Tibetan political leader, years in which he included all branches of monastic life incorporating representatives of the Bon religion within the Tibetan Parliament on exile.

In his teachings of chapter 9 of the *Bodhicharyāvatāra*, the Dalai Lama acknowledged the arrival of the *dharma* from India and the first of the four schools, the Nyingma, as the 'old translation' school, which started at the time of Padmasambhava.[53] Padmasambhava, born in Udyāna (Swat, Pakistan), came from a place of magicians, was a member of the Yogācāra and taught at Nalanda, a centre of Buddhist studies in India. He was invited to Tibet in 747 by King Thī-srong-detsan. Since that time other three traditions, called 'new translations' by the Dalai Lama evolved, namely the Kagyü, Sakya, and Geluk.[54] Four of them are for the non-sectarian as the Dalai Lama 'complete forms of Buddhism' as they contain the essence of the teachings of the Hinayana with every lineage containing the essence of the Mahāyāna and Vajrayana Buddhism.

For the Dalai Lama, it is the *dharma* as the teaching that leads to wisdom, a reflection that sometimes has not been emphasized enough, and that needs to be outlined as totally complementary and significant in relation to the acquiring *of bodhichitta*, stressed within chapter 3 of the *Bodhicharyāvatāra*. Thus, chapter 9 of the *Bodhicharyāvatāra*, according to Khenpo Künpal and Minyak Künso, is divided into three segments: the necessity of cultivating the wisdom of emptiness (verse 1), a detailed explanation of how to cultivate this wisdom (verses 2–150), and a concise explanation of how to realize emptiness (verses 151–167).[55] Verse 1 constitutes a reminder that all teachings of the Buddha have an intention to reach full enlightenment; all teachings are aimed at generating wisdom and for gaining wisdom.[56] Within such reminder the Dalai Lama remarked that within the *Bodhicharyāvatāra* the realization of emptiness is indispensable so that when we speak of freedom from suffering we also include the origins of suffering, i.e. afflictive emotions and thoughts, and not just painful sensations.[57] Therefore, the whole second section of chapter 9 constitutes a long explanation on how to achieve the realization of emptiness.

The second section brings the mastery of Shantideva's understanding of the realization of emptiness whereby chapter 9 brings the two truths, a reality defined and contested by different authors, but that Shantideva, following Tsong-Kha-Pa, assumes as the 'ultimate reality', as not being within the reach of the intellect, and ultimately providing the definition of 'ultimate truth'.[58] Shantideva defined 'ultimate truth' as the aspect of reality in which dualistic cognition is relative and conditional, thus defining the two truths (9.2).[59] Thus, definitions within *tantra* are different but in Shantideva's understanding the two truths include all things and events, and there is nothing in reality that cannot be contained in the two truths; there is no third possibility.[60] The two truths share the same reality as adhered to in the *Heart Sutra*, as stated by the Buddha 'form is emptiness, emptiness is form'.[61] Indeed, such teachings and understanding return to the basics of Buddhism as outlined by the Dalai Lama in the 'Introduction' to his *Commentary* where he argued that 'underlying its entire spiritual path is the premise that there is a profound disparity between our perceptions of reality and the ways things really are'.[62] The antidote of ignorance is, of course, knowledge, that widens our perspectives and makes us more familiar with the world.[63] In the spiritual path, the same rules apply so that knowledge overcomes ignorance and suffering and the two truths are fully embraced by those who follow the path of Buddhism towards enlightenment.

In conclusion to this period of monastic formation in Tibet one could argue that the preparation of the Dalai Lama was the best he could have had at that time within the confines of Tibet, and within a Tibet that was still not open to other peoples and worlds, despite the challenges of the periodic arrival of merchants and the threat of foreign powers. However, the roots of the Dalai Lama's political philosophy as peacekeeping were there in the *Bodhicharyāvatāra*, and an evaluation of his actions would suggest that he did not compromise those values. On the contrary, he emphasised them globally. Thus, his flight into exile in India provided a continuity as well as a discontinuity of his Buddhist education in Tibet in which he was able to return to his Indian Buddhist roots. It was also a learning project of political management within an exile in which he needed to speak for his own Tibetan people. He had been taught how to lead the Tibetan government within Tibet, and he had to learn and develop ways of establishing a Tibetan government in exile without ignoring Buddhist values and the traditions of Tibet.

A short historical mention is in order here. The Dalai Lama was very aware while in Tibet that if Tibet has to overcome the failing of a feudal system and its isolation, Tibetans would have to collaborate and learn from outsiders, something that was feared particularly by the Abbotts of the major Geluk monasteries. Thus, during the period before exile he spent time with Europeans who visited Lhasa and developed an interest in science outside Tibet. For example, Heinrich Harrer (1912–2006), an Austrian mountaineer, who lived in Lhasa because of World War II, met the Dalai Lama when his holiness was 11 years of age. Harrer translated some English writings for the Dalai Lama and taught Tibetans how to use some of the cinema equipment, BBC recordings, and astronomical equipment given to the 13th Dalai Lama.[64] Another major influence was the British diplomat Hugh Richardson (1905–2000), born in St. Andrews, Scotland, who studied at Keble College, Oxford, and entered the Indian Civil Service in October 1930. He represented Britain in Lhasa from 1936 to 1940, and British India and independent India from 1946 to 1950. He spoke Bengali and Tibetan, and he became an accomplished Tibetologist as well as an international campaigner for the rights of Tibet.[65]

Later, and on exile, the Dalai Lama was able to develop such awareness of a global humanity through projects of Tibetan knowledge and Western science, for example the cooperation of the Dalai Lama's Foundation with Emory University, outlined in the last chapter (Chapter 5) of this work. Such a delayed interest in the non-Tibetan world can be described as a process of verification that he later encouraged in all those interested in Buddhism so as 'to analyse and investigate whether we are seeing things as they truly are'.[66]

Notes

1 Some of those texts were destroyed by the Chinese invasion of Tibet and others were translated and restored by contemporary scholars after they were collected by the British Library; see, for example, the collection of ancient Gandhāra texts in Richard Salomon, *The Buddhist Literature of Ancient Gandhāra: An Introduction with*

Selected Translations. Somerville, MA: Wisdom Publications, 2018.

2 Thomas Laird, *The Story of Tibet: Conversations with the Dalai Lama*. London: Atlantic Books, 2006, p. 281. An original video of the Dalai Lama's public examination that took place at Ganden Monastery in the summer of 1958 is available at https://www.youtube.com/watch?v=hbnKkuYR3Jk&t=29s Accessed 15 May 2020.

3 See the complexity of the development of monasteries within the history of Tibet in Mario I. Aguilar, '*Densa Sum, Sendregasum*, and the Three Seats: The Role of Gelugpa Monasteries in Tibet (1409–1959)', *The Tibet Journal* XL/1, 2015, pp. 23–40.

4 The Dalai Lama, *My Land and My People*. New York: McGraw-Hill, 1962. For some of the ideas on the Tibetan natural and scientific world see for example Thupten Jinpa, ed., *Science and Philosophy in the Indian Buddhist Classics*, Volume I: The Physical World. Somerville, MA: Wisdom Publications, 2017.

5 Laird, *The Story of Tibet*, p. 125.

6 Vicki Mackenzie, *The Revolutionary Life of Freda Bedi: British Feminist, Indian Nationalist, Buddhist Nun*. Boulder, CO: Shambala Publications, 2017.

7 https://www.nobelprize.org/prizes/peace/1989/lama/facts/

8 See the Dalai Lama's initial assessments of his exit from Lhasa and exile in India in 'Into Exile: Statement to the Press', Tezpur, 18 April 1959, and 'Tragedy in Crimson: Statement to the Press', Mussoorie, 20 June 1959, in Subhash C. Kashyap, *The Political Philosophy of the Dalai Lama: Selected Speeches and Writings*. New Delhi: Rupa Publications India Pvt. Ltd, 2014, pp. 3–5, 6–9.

9 *The Great Treatise on the Stages of the Path to Enlightenment*, 3 vols. Ithaca, NY: Snow Lion Publications, 2001, 2002, 2004.

10 Geshe Thupten Wangyal, *The Door of Liberation: Essential Teachings of the Tibetan Buddhist Tradition*. Somerville, MA: Wisdom Publications, 1998, and Anne Carolyn Klein and Geshe Tenzin Wangyal Rinpoche, *Unbounded Wholeness: Dzochen, Bon, and the Logic of the Nonconceptual*. New York: Oxford University Press, 2006.

11 The Dalai Lama, *From Here to Enlightenment: An Introduction to Tsong-Kha-Pa's Classic Text the Great Treatise on the Stages of the Path to Enlightenment*. Boston, MA and London: Snow Lion, 2013.

12 Within this work I use the translation by the Padmakara Translation Group published as Shantideva, *The Way of the Bodhisattva*. Boston, MA and London: Shambala, 2006, abbreviated throughout this chapter as *Bodhicharyāvatāra*.

13 The Dalai Lama's commentary on the *Bodhicharyāvatāra* was published as Tenzin Yatso the Fourteenth Dalai Lama, *For the Benefit of All Human Beings: A Commentary on the Way of the Bodhisattva*. Boston, MA and London: Shambala, 2009, abbreviated throughout this chapter as *Commentary*. The November 1993 teachings at Lavaur, France, where he taught chapter 9 of *Bodhicharyāvatāra* were later published as *Practicing Wisdom*. Somerville, MA: Wisdom Publications, 2004.

14 Tulku Pema Wangyal, 'Foreword', in *Commentary*, p. vii.

15 The Dalai Lama, 'The Tibetan Conundrum: New Delhi, 5 September 1959', in Subhash C. Kashyap (ed). *The Political Philosophy of the Dalai Lama*, pp. 10–11 at p. 10.

16 The Dalai Lama has emphasized the need to treat the *Bodhicharyāvatāra* as a means 'to progress spiritually' rather than as an academic subject, even for those who teach it to others, see *Commentary*, p. 1.

17 *Commentary*, p. 2.

18 *Commentary*, p. 3.

19 *Commentary*, p. 3.

20 *Commentary*, p. 3.

21 *Commentary*, p. 4.

22 *Commentary*, p. 4.

23 *Commentary*, p. 4.

24 *Commentary*, p. 4.

25 *Commentary*, p. 4.

26 *Commentary*, pp. 4–5.

27 'Introduction' to Shantideva, *The Way of the Bodhisattva*. Boston, MA and London: Shambala, 2006, p. 2.

28 *Bodhicharyāvatāra* 3.1.

29 *The Way of the Bodhisattva* note 45 at p. 200.

30 *The Way of the Bodhisattva* note 45 at p. 200; see also Donald S. Lopez Jr., *Seeing the Sacred in Samsara: An Illustrated Guide to the Eighty-Four Mahasiddhas*. Boston, MA: Shambala Publications, 2019, and Ben Meulenbeld, *Buddhist Symbolism in Tibetan Thangkas: The Story of Shiddharta and Other Buddhas Interpreted in Modern Nepalese Painting*. Haarlem, Low Countries: Binkey Kok Publications, 2001.

31 *Bodhicharyāvatāra* 3.5.

32 *Bodhicharyāvatāra* 3.6.

33 *The Way of the Bodhisattva*, note 48 at p. 200, cf. Kate Crosby and Andrew Skilton, trans. *The Bodhicaryāvatāra*. Translated from the Sanskrit. Oxford: Oxford University Press, 1996.

34 *Bodhicharyāvatāra* 3.7.

35 *Bodhicharyāvatāra* 3.8.

36 *Bodhicharyāvatāra* 3.9, cf. *The Way of the Bodhisattva* note 49 at p. 200.

37 *Bodhicharyāvatāra* 3.10.
38 *Bodhicharyāvatāra* 3.10.
39 *Bodhicharyāvatāra* 3.11.
40 *Bodhicharyāvatāra* 3.12.
41 *Bodhicharyāvatāra* 3.13–14.
42 *Bodhicharyāvatāra* 3.15.
43 *Bodhicharyāvatāra* 3.17.
44 *Bodhicharyāvatāra* 3.18.
45 *Bodhicharyāvatāra* 3.19.
46 *Bodhicharyāvatāra* 3.24.
47 Thumten Jinpa, 'Editor's Preface', in The Dalai Lama, *Practicing Wisdom: The Perfection of Shantideva's Bodhisattva Way*. Edited and translated by Thupten Jinpa. Somerville, MA: Wisdom Publications, 2005, pp. vii–xiii at p. ix.
48 The Dalai Lama, *Practicing Wisdom*, 'Chapter Three: The Two Truths', pp. 16–30.
49 Tsonkhapa, 'Notes on the Wisdom Chapter', in *The Collected Works of Tsongkhapa*, vol. *pha* (14) [Tibetan text].
50 Thupten Jinpa, 'Editor's Preface' to *Practising Wisdom*, pp. vii–xiii at p. xii.
51 Mipham Jamyang Namgyal Gyatso, 'Exposition of the Ornament of the Middle Way (*dbu ma rgyan gyi rnam bshad*)', in *The Collected Works of Ju Mipham*, vol. *nga* (4).
52 The Dalai Lama, *Practicing Wisdom*, p. 4; cf. Khenpo Künsang Palden, *Sacred Words of My Teacher Manjushri* (*byang chub sems dpa'i spyod pa la 'jug pa rtsa ba dang 'grel pa*), typeset edition. Chengdu, Sichuan; Xinhua, Hunan: National Minorities Press, 1990, and Minyak Künsang Sönam, *Brilliant Lamp Illuminating the Suchness of Profound Dependent Origination* (*spyod 'jug gi 'grel bshad rgyal sras yon tan bum bzang*), typeset edition. Xinhua: National Minorities Press, 1990.
53 The Dalai Lama, *Practicing Wisdom*, p. 6.
54 The Dalai Lama, *Practicing Wisdom*, p. 6.
55 The Dalai Lama, *Practicing Wisdom*, p. 16.
56 The Dalai Lama, *Practicing Wisdom*, p. 17.
57 The Dalai Lama, *Practicing Wisdom*, p. 17.
58 The Dalai Lama, *Practicing Wisdom*, p. 20.
59 The Dalai Lama, *Practicing Wisdom*, p. 20.
60 The Dalai Lama, *Practicing Wisdom*, p. 21.
61 The Dalai Lama, *Practicing Wisdom*, p. 23; cf. Tenzin Gyatso the Fourteenth Dalai Lama, *Essence of the Heart Sutra: The Dalai Lama's Heart of Wisdom Teachings*. Translated and edited by Geshe Thupten Jinpa. Somerville, MA: Wisdom Publications, 2005, 2015.
62 The Dalai Lama, *Practicing Wisdom*, p. 6.
63 The Dalai Lama, *Practicing Wisdom*, p. 7.

64 John Gittings, 'Obituary: Heinrich Harrer', *The Guardian*, 9 January 2006 at https://www.theguardian.com/news/2006/jan/09/guardianobituaries.johngittings Accessed 17 May 2020; and Heinrich Harrer, *Sieben Jahre in Tibet: mein Leben am Hofe des Dalai Lama*. Vienna: Ullstein, 1952, *Return to Tibet*. New York: Schocken Books, 1985, and *Lost Lhasa: Heinrich Harrer Tibet*. New York, NY: Harry N. Abrams Inc., 1992.

65 Hugh E. Richardson, *A Corpus of Early Tibetan Inscriptions*. London: Royal Asiatic Society, 1985, Michael Aris, ed., *Ceremonies of the Lhasa Year*, London: Serinda, 1993, and, *High Peaks, Pure Earth: Collected Writings on Tibetan Culture and History*, edited with an introduction by Michael Aris. London: Serindia, 1998.

66 The Dalai Lama, *For the Benefit of All Beings*, p. 121.

3

EXILE AND EXTERNAL PEACEBUILDING

The Buddhist formation of a Dalai Lama prepared the 14th Dalai Lama for a ritual and political office in Tibet. However, the crisis in 1959 that triggered his exit from Lhasa was a completely new development.[1] He was young and therefore inexperienced on the art of diplomacy within the Tibetan government. His first peacekeeping exercise was the decision to remain with his people in Tibet until March 1959, which he conveyed to Indian Prime Minister Jawaharlal Nehru, and his second peacekeeping exercise was his decision to exit Tibet and travel to India after this, his oracle advised him to leave. His international envoys were clear in that India and other European countries would support him, but that they could not antagonise the Chinese as to prevent their actions in Tibet. India was the Dalai Lama's first choice because he could just cross the border, even with a long journey crossing the mountains, but knowing that India was the land of the Buddha. Hindus in India consider him an avatar of the gods as the incarnation of former spiritual masters, and therefore India was and is at the forefront of administrative support for the Tibetan community in exile. One could argue that it was the exit into India that made the Dalai Lama into an international political leader because he had to negotiate for the first time the survival of Tibetans outside Tibet and within a post-independence India. The Mongols were not there to protect Tibet and Indian Prime Minister Nehru had discussed the possibility of such exile already in 1956 when the Dalai Lama had visited India. The Dalai Lama had visited India for the 2,500th anniversary of the Buddha's enlightenment and at that time he was ready to seek asylum in India; however, Prime Minister Jawaharlal Nehru convinced him to return to Tibet after Chinese Premier Zhou Enlai gave assurances that Tibet's autonomy would be respected.[2]

The events that followed were the Chinese invasion of Tibet that started in 1950 and culminated with the flight of the 14th Dalai Lama into exile made the head of the Geluk into a universal figure of peacebuilding. Indeed, one could have assumed a different outcome to the Dalai Lama's engagement with the world after the Chinese invasion. For one could argue that if the Dalai Lama would have not been a Buddhist monk, he could have attempted to gather a large army outside Tibet to return and free Tibet from the Chinese occupation by force. Further, he could have assigned further autonomy and strength to the Kampa fighters who with the help of the Central Intelligence Agency (CIA) of the United States remained as interested parties within Tibet. The making of a Dalai Lama as head of state was clearly that of a peacemaker, suggesting at any given moment that the fate of Tibetans was in the hands of a peaceful negotiation with China rather than on any armed conflict within Tibet. There is no doubt that the Dalai Lama learned the lessons of diplomatic co-existence from Buddhist inter-dependency and his own lessons of exile rather than the lessons of armed conflict from the Mongols.

Exile and a school of peacebuilding

When the 14th Dalai Lama had to decide whether to leave Lhasa or remain within Tibet at the time of the Chinese occupation of March 1959 he consulted his personal oracle several times as well as keeping a conversation going with his religious and political advisors.[3] However, the decision to leave was taken immediately after his oracle had indicated that he should go to India. On 16 March 1959 he consulted the Nechung Oracle and in his words 'the oracle made it clear that I should stay and keep open the dialogue with the Chinese'.[4] On 17 March 1959 the oracle

shouted 'Go! Go! Tonight!' and the Dalai Lama recalled the
event in his autobiography as follows:

> The medium, still in his trance, then staggered forward
> and, snatching up some paper and a pen, wrote down,
> quite clearly and explicitly, the route that I should take
> out of the Norbulingka, down to the last Tibetan town
> on the Indian border [...] That done, the medium, a young
> monk named Lobsang Jigme, collapsed in a faint, signi-
> fying that Dorje Drakden had left his body. Just then, as
> if to reinforce the oracle's instructions, two mortar shells
> exploded in the marsh outside the northern gate of the
> Jewel Park.[5]

It is clear that in the 14th Dalai Lama's conversations with the
American writer Thomas Laird he warned Laird about his understanding of history, coming out of Buddhist philosophy, as
two-folded, so that facts and intentions, material realities and
spiritual causations, what happened and his own interpretation
of what could have happened make decisions possible rather than
a single material reality. Laird recorded such initial conversation
as follows:

> So there are two viewpoints, one common and one un-
> common. The uncommon viewpoint is not considered
> history, because historians cannot record these things.
> But we cannot say that all such things are just the imag-
> ination of the Buddhist faithful. They can also be true.[6]

Robert Ekvall has argued that a Tibetan philosophy of history
points to central moments that allow an understanding of religious centralization as a mediating force in international relations so that 'a philosophy of history not only explains the past
but provides a frame of reference for evaluating current historical
developments', thus 'the end of the Manchu dynasty broke, for
the Tibetans, a special tie that existed between the emperor, as
imperial secular ruler, and his religious chaplain, the Dalai Lama,

and the religious system of which he was the head'.[7] This diverse understanding of history must be kept in mind when trying to understand the Dalai Lama's efforts for peacebuilding not only between Tibet and China but also in other parts of the world.

On 7 October 1950 Chinese troops had started their attack on the eastern Tibetan border helped by the Khampa, feudal warriors from across the Yangtze. The Khampa had symbolic and ritual allegiance to the Dalai Lama but did not trust the centralised bureaucracy in Lhasa and were happy to get rid of them. The Chinese promised them an independent eastern Tibet and very quickly eastern Tibet fell into the hands of the incoming troops with two prominent foreigners involved in the ordeal: Geoffrey Bull was a missionary on the east side of the upper Yangtse and Robert Ford operated the Tibetan government's wireless station at Chambdo. Both of them were taken prisoners and had the experience of the Chinese interrogation and re-education methods and their tales of suffering alerted the Western world of the methods used by the Chinese army in securing an absolute control of all of China.[8]

Robert Ford was taken prisoner and after months of interrogation he was accused of killing somebody, accusation that he always denied. During his time in prison he was able to witness the crushing of the eastern Tibetans and their re-education into agreeing that they had been oppressed by the Dalai Lama and that Mao's policies would bring prosperity and freedom to the whole of Tibet. Ford was a prisoner of the Chinese for a few years and in 1954 he was allowed to write to his parents in England to tell them that he was alive but through a letter format in which he praised the new Chinese society that was being shaped by Chairman Mao.[9] However, in Ford's writings it was clear that at that time the Chinese were not destroying monasteries or material culture with religious significance but they were interested in bringing back Tibet to the Chinese motherland. Ford wrote:

> There was no sacking of monasteries this time. On the contrary, the Chinese took care not to cause offense through ignorance. They soon had the monks thanking the gods for their deliverance. The Chinese had made it clear that they had no quarrel with the Tibetan religion.[10]

While the Chinese attack on the east was expected there was also a smaller fighting force that crossed the Kuen Lun Mountains and passing through the Indian territory entered north-west Tibet, taking everybody by surprise. News from eastern Tibet were not forthcoming as the wireless station was in Chinese hands; however, news of the Chinese invasion was circulated all over the world. The Indian government sent a note of protest arguing that force was not the way to solve the problem and further stressing the fact that the use of force could compromise the acceptance of the new Chinese government into the international forum of members of the United Nations. On 26 October 1950, the Indian government once again expressed its regret that questions about the use of force were being ignored by the Chinese government. The Chinese response was different than in the past – it was blunt and clear: Tibet belonged to China and was being treated as a domestic problem that did not merit any foreign intervention by India or anybody else. The Chinese army had entered Tibet, the note said, in order to liberate Tibet and to protect China's frontiers.[11] Finally, the note to the Indian government indicated that India's position had been tainted by foreign influence. The Indian government was clearly taken back by this accusation and in a reply dated 31 October 1950 protested against such opinion stating that it was possible for China to relate to an autonomous Tibet under the accepted terms of 'Chinese suzerainty' and that the Chinese attack on Tibet had been unprovoked. China accused India of trying to interfere with claims that were part of Chinese sovereignty. The Indian government did not reply. In the meantime, the Chinese attack on Tibet was discussed at the British Parliament and on 6 November 1950. Ernest Davies expressed support for the Indian government, recalling the assurances given to Britain about the autonomy of Tibet in 1947.

On 6 November 1950, the Tibetan government appealed to the United Nations stating clearly that Tibetans did not want to be part of China and that the use of force amounted to a clear Chinese aggression against Tibet. The United Kingdom and India were not helpful in the United Nations and it was the delegate from El Salvador who proceeded to move a motion condemning the Chinese invasion of Tibet. The British delegate pleaded ignorance and requested that any discussion on the motion should be deferred. The Indian government seconded the motion arguing that matters could be settled without a condemnation of China and that the autonomy of Tibet was not being jeopardised. The Chinese nationalists and the Soviet Union supported the Communists by dismissing the motion. The United States agreed to end any discussions on account of the Indian government's position and thus the discussion ended after another nine years.

The Tibetan government was astonished, and it still sent two telegrams to the United Nations. In one of them dated 11 December 1950 the Tibetan government requested the appointment of a fact-finding mission; it never got an answer. Even when the Chinese halted their advance from eastern Tibet the situation was very critical and the Dalai Lama, still sixteen years of age, was invested with ruling powers. However, after consulting with his oracle he decided to leave Lhasa. Together with a small entourage of government officials he travelled to the Chumbi valley from where he could have crossed into India at any given time. It was crucial that the Chinese did not have the possibility of holding the Dalai Lama prisoner while negotiations between China and Tibet took place. The negotiations lasted for four months in which the captive minister Ngabo, governor of Chambo, negotiated the terms of a political solution with the Chinese government of Peking. In April 1951, a Tibetan delegation led by Ngabo, who was already a Chinese collaborator, headed for Peking to pursue further negotiations on the Tibetan borders. On 23 May 1951 Ngabo and the Chinese officials signed an agreement that allowed 'the peaceful liberation of Tibet'.

The agreement of 23 May 1951 with the title 'Agreement on Measures for the Peaceful Liberation of Tibet', also known as the 17-point agreement, was signed by the Tibetans left with no choice but to sign whatever was put to them as the Chinese Army was already in Tibet and could have continued its advance by force.[12] The agreement laid down very clearly the annexation of Tibet by China but promised to respect religious freedom, the authority of the Dalai Lama, the Panchen Lama, and the Tibetan local authorities; see for example paragraphs (1), (4), and (7):

(1) The Tibetan people shall unite and drive out imperialist aggressive forces from Tibet; the Tibetan people shall return to the big family of the Motherland – the People's Republic of China.

(4) The central authorities will not alter the existing political system in Tibet. The central authorities also will not alter the established status, functions, and powers of the Dalai Lama. Officials of various ranks shall hold office as usual.

(7) The policy of freedom of religious belief laid down in the Common Programme of the Chinese People's Political Consultative Conference (CPPCC) shall be carried out. The religious beliefs, customs and habits of the Tibetan people shall be respected, and lama monasteries shall be protected. The central authorities will not affect a change in the income of the monasteries.[13]

In July 1952, the Chinese General Chang Ching-Wu, appointed Commissioner and Administrator of Civil and Military Affairs in Tibet, travelled to India and had a meeting with the Dalai Lama in the Chumbi valley. He requested that the Dalai Lama return to Lhasa, a request that was reinforced by many monks. The Dalai Lama returned to Lhasa and witnessed the military occupation by 3,000 troops in Lhasa and 20,000 more all over Tibet. The building up of troops continued as new roads were built between China and Tibet and several new airstrips were constructed as to accommodate both the trucks transporting troops as well as the ongoing air network between China and Tibet. By 1951 after the first Chinese invasion of Tibet, Drepung Monastery officially recognised a community of 7,700 monks while the monastic community most probably accounted for 10,000 monks. Sera Monastery held 5,500 (7,000) monks and Ganden Monastery 3,300 (5,000). The number of monks in Lhasa was higher than the Tibetan army, which had 1,000 or 1,500 troops. The monasteries developed over the years the category of fighting monks (*dobdos*), monks that had a particular appearance with distinctive hair and a different way of tying their robes; they also belonged to athletic associations that held competitions regularly. The *dobdos* engaged in ritualised fighting and acted as bodyguards for the monastery.[14] The possibilities for armed conflict between the monasteries and the Tibetan government at that time cannot be underestimated as the number of fighting monks and the number of monks in general was larger than the actual Tibetan army. The Three Seats were also connected to other monasteries throughout the country; thus, an issue relevant to the Lhasa monasteries had at any given time the support of other monasteries throughout Tibet.

The importance of Ganden can be shown by the fact that the 14th Dalai Lama visited Ganden before his departure from Tibet in 1959 as well as taking his final examinations through debating at Ganden in 1958.[15] At that time the monastery twenty four chapels with large statues of the Buddha and the biggest chapel seated 3,500 monks during rituals.[16] One of the temples housed Tsong Khapa's tomb, decorated with gold; however, during the cultural revolution of the 1960s Chinese soldiers destroyed Ganden forcing a monk, Bomi Rimpoché, to carry the mummy to a burning fire.[17] Later the monk saved the skull and some ashes and the reconstruction of Tsong Khapa's tomb began in the 1980s after the end of the period known as the Cultural Revolution in China and Tibet.[18]

By then, and according to approximate figures provided by a government survey of the 1950s there were approximately 90,000 monks in Tibet; but a larger figure, of up to 120,000 monks in 2,700 monasteries, was given in another survey mentioned by the Tibet Academy of Social Sciences.[19] The number of monks serving as government officials amounted to hundreds. Thus, when the 14th Dalai Lama left Lhasa for India in March 1959, after the rising of women who feared that the Dalai Lama would be taken prisoner and the bombardment of Lhasa on 10 March 1959, he most probably felt that Tibetan history was unfolding towards an uncertain future. On his way to India the total autonomy of Tibet was declared, and as Chinese troops came closer, the independent flags of Tibet sealed such manifesto of autonomy with the presence of the Dalai Lama who represented Tibet wherever he was. He made it to the Indian border, ill and weak, being welcomed with his companions by the government of India.

Diplomatic peacebuilding

As China took control of Tibet the Tibetan government on exile had several immediate tasks: to settle exiles that kept arriving in India, to start programmes of education, relief, and cultural awareness, and to seek help from the international community in order to rescue Tibet and Tibetans from full destruction by China. It is here that the young Dalai Lama grew in stature in a role for which he was not prepared. The wish for return and for Tibetan independence was there but he quickly realized that very few actors in the world were going to be present to march with the Dalai Lama back to Lhasa. The Cold War between the United States and the Soviet Union was dominating international relations and China remained closed to the outside world. India was building democracy after independence and it was not the internationally powerful India of today. The Tibetan community in India finally settled their Dalai Lama and their government on the hills of Dharamshala in northern India, and the community remained grateful to Prime Minister Nehru who welcomed them to India and laid the foundations for programmes of education and rehabilitation of a community on exile.[20]

In the early 1970s the Dalai Lama decided with his senior officials, using Buddhist language, to put forward his middle-way approach.[21] Within such a peaceful approach the autonomy, religious and cultural heritage of Tibet was of central importance. Thus, later the Dalai Lama made explicit a resolution of the Tibet issue that did not call for independence or its separation from China any longer.[22] The Dalai Lama emphasized his belief that a political solution could be found with the survival of the spiritual heritage of Tibet, namely compassion and non-violence.[23] The Dalai Lama saw compassion and non-violence as Tibet's contribution to the contemporary world, and in late 1978, Deng Xiaoping resumed dialogue with the Dalai Lama regarding the question of Tibet, and this dialogue came to an end in August 1993. The Chinese government settled the question without dialogue as they moved into a new era of international politics as a united China with Tibet as part of such political unit. Events that preceded to break the dialogue included the signing of a friendly treaty between China and Russia in 1992, and the change of Chinese premier in 1993 when Jiang Zemin replaced Yan Shangkun. However, Tibetan envoys and Chinese officials maintained a flow of conversations over the years aided by foreign dignitaries such as President Clinton who discussed the Tibetan question with the Chinese premier during his visit to China in June 1998.[24] The visit was extremely important as it happened after nine years without a visit to China by a U.S. President after the crushing of the protestors in Tiananmen Square in 1989.[25] President Clinton made the issue of Taiwan central to the visit but at the same time spoke of issues regarding Tiananmen Square and Tibet on that meeting held on 27 June 1998 in the Great Hall of the People.[26]

After the end of a public dialogue about Tibet and despite the efforts by President Clinton the Dalai Lama recognised in 2000 that the 'strike hard' and 'patriotic re-education' campaigns by China and within China had intensified.[27] Those campaigns against Tibetan religion and patriotism resembled, according to the Dalai Lama, the days of the Cultural Revolution.[28] Further, the Dalai Lama recognised that a very worrying trend was the increased movement of Chinese settlers into Tibet with an increase in gambling places, prostitution, and karaoke bars, all social phenomenon opposed to the traditional social norms and spiritual values of Tibet.[29] The Dalai Lama reiterated on Tibet Uprising Day 2000 his wish to find a peaceful and mutually acceptable solution to the Tibetan problem by stating 'I remain committed to the process of dialogue'.[30] Of course, due to breakdown of dialogue with China the Dalai Lama did not have any other choice than to appeal for help to foster this possible dialogue within members of the international community.[31]

One of the most difficult issues within the ongoing peacekeeping in Tibetan issues vis-à-vis China, the international community, and the young Tibetan community has been the very office and person of the Dalai Lama.[32] As early as 1969 the Dalai Lama made clear that it was up to the Tibetan people if the 'very institution of the Dalai Lama which is over three hundred years old should continue or not.'[33] In 1992 the Dalai Lama had stated in a policy position paper that if Tibetans were to return to Tibet with some degree of freedom he would not have held any position in the Tibetan government.[34] In this visionary statement he was advancing his actions of 2011 when he renounced any right to any political power, and forced the Tibetan community to have fully democratic elections throughout the world. He had assumed political leadership at the age of sixteen, at an age when he admitted that 'at that time I lacked a thorough understanding of Tibet's own political system, let alone international affairs.'[35] Since 1959, several reforms within the Tibetan Parliament and government had allowed democratic reforms, particularly through the establishment of the Charter for Tibetans in Exile in 1990 and an increase of the total number of members of the Assembly of Tibetan People's Deputies (ATPD), the highest law-making body for Tibetans in exile in 1991.[36] In 2001 Tibetans elected the Kalon Tripa, their political leader, directly, for the first time.[37] It was on 14 March 2011 that the Dalai Lama asked the Tibetan Parliament in Exile to amend the Charter and to make all other necessary regulations during the sitting of 2011 for him to be 'completely relieved of formal authority'.[38] A few days later the Dalai Lama made other important remarks regarding the end of his political authority by suggesting that 'since the direct election of the Kalon Tripa, the system of the institution of Gaden Phodrang of the Dalai Lama as both the spiritual and temporal authority has ended'.[39] Further, he emphasised that the rule of kings and religious leaders was outdated adding that 'we have to follow the trend of the free world which is that of democracy'.[40] The worries by Tibetans were understandable but the Dalai Lama assured them that he would lead them spiritually for the rest of his life.[41]

Following the changes requested to the Tibetan Parliament on exile, Dr Lobsang Sangay was sworn in as the new Kalon Tripa in Dharamshala on 12 August 2011. During the ceremony, the Dalai Lama spoke about a proud moment for Tibetans who had worked hard to conduct this election among the different Tibetan communities throughout the world. However, he discouraged personal fame and fortune within Tibet's life-and-death struggle.[42]

The Dalai Lama's succession

By fostering dialogue with China at all times the Dalai Lama managed to act as a peacekeeper between radical elements that wanted to carry out guerrilla warfare in Tibet and the strong proposers of the closing of all monasteries within the Chinese Communist Party. The greatest challenge to his authority after he left political power in 2011 came with the ongoing crisis of Tibetan immolations. Immolations took place in Tibet, India, and Nepal and they started with the immolation of Tapey, a Kirti monk, who set himself on fire when prayers were cancelled at his monastery (Kirti, Ngaba Tibetan and Qiang Autonomous Prefecture, Sichuan province) on 27 February 2009. However, the wave of immolations started in 2011.[43] The act of immolation is a public manifestation of control over one's body and of martyrdom for a cause. As outlined by Plank it has to be understood within a larger set of practices called 'gift of the body', and the 1960s acts of immolation in order to save Buddhism in South Vietnam and to end the Vietnam War gained international interest.[44] However, in the case of Tibetan immolations, what appeared to be isolated incidents by individuals at the beginning of the immolations continued as a practice that attracted international attention to the plight of Tibetan cultural and religious autonomy. The Dalai Lama remained neutral in his general comments regarding immolations and during his visit to Okinawa, Japan, in November 2012, he reminded his audience that he had retired from political responsibility.[45] However, he reminded his audience that the immolations were the symptoms of a larger problem, rather than a problem created by Tibetans in exile or the Dalai Lama. Throughout the immolation crisis the Dalai Lama has been respectful of the suffering and pain of the families of those who immolated themselves but has not approved of such actions.

The changes within the Tibetan political leadership took place amid an international preoccupation for the Tibetan self-immolations. And while the issue of the Dalai Lama's role as spiritual leader of the Tibetan community seemed to be settled, further public noises were made by the Chinese and the Tibetans regarding the next Dalai Lama and the very nature of the Gaden Phodrang Labrang (the Dalai Lama's institution). Since 1642 and the government of the Great Fifth, the Dalai Lama had also been the political leader of Tibet. On 14 September 2011 the 14th Dalai Lama having renounced any political power warned about the manipulation of his reincarnation for other purposes than spiritual leadership and guidance.[46] Thus, the Dalai Lama decided that it was necessary to draw clear guidelines in order to choose the next Dalai Lama by understanding the system of Tulku recognition and the basic concepts behind it.[47] While the Dalai Lama summarizes the whole issue of reincarnation within Buddhism in a very complex manner the reincarnation of the Dalai Lama relates to the Tulkus vis-à-vis the Incarnate Emanation Body, whereby 'Buddhas appear in various forms such as human beings, deities, rivers, bridges, medicinal plants, and trees to help sentient beings'.[48] Tulkus fall within this category of Incarnate Emanation Bodies of the Buddha, or reincarnations of 'superior Bodhisattva, Bodhisattvas on the path of accumulation and preparation, as well as masters who are evidently yet to enter the Bodhisattva paths'.[49]

Past and future lives were part of the Tibetan indigenous Bon religion, and since Buddhism arrived in Tibet past and future lives have been central to Tibetan Buddhism.[50] Such system of present recognition with numbering started with the recognition of Karmapa Pagshi as the reincarnation of Karmapa Dusum Khyenpa by his disciples. Since then there have been seventeen Karmapa incarnations. Among the Tulkus there have been monastic and lay tantric practitioners, male and female.[51] There are also recognised Tulkus in all Tibetan Buddhist traditions, i.e. the Sakya, Geluk, Kagyu, and Nyingma, and in other traditions such as Jonang and Bodong.

The Dalai Lama stated that there were different traditional methods for the recognition of a Dalai Lama since the priest–patron relationship between Tibet and the Manchus ended. He expressed his worry about the Chinese interference with the appointment of the 15th Dalai Lama, particularly since the so-called Order No. Five concerning the Chinese government's control and recognition of reincarnations came into force on 1 September 2007.[52] Thus, the Dalai Lama's declaration came as his duty to protect the Dharma and sentient beings.[53] In its final and practical instructions the Dalai Lama outlined a fact in Tibetan Buddhism: reincarnation takes place through the voluntary choice of the concerned person or on the strength of his or her *karma*, merit, and prayers.[54] Thus, the Dalai Lama continued, it is the person who reincarnates who has sole legitimate authority over where and how that reincarnation is to be recognised. The Dalai Lama's announcement in September 2011 was clear: when he becomes ninety years of age or so he would consult high Lamas in the Tibetan tradition, as well as the Tibetan public, and others who follow the Tibetan Buddhism, in order to re-evaluate if the institution of the Dalai Lama should continue or not. If the decision is for such institution to continue the recognition of the Dalai Lama will be left to the officers of the Dalai Lama's Gaden Phodrang Trust, Heads of all the Tibetan Buddhist traditions as well as the oath-bound Dharma Protectors linked to the Dalai Lamas' lineage. They should follow past procedures within the Tibetan tradition and instructions would be left by the 14th Dalai Lama. Finally, the Dalai Lama stated clearly that no recognition or acceptance should be given to anybody chosen for political ends by the People's Republic of China.[55]

From Tibet to the world

With his resignation from political office the Dalai Lama allowed himself to cancel the visits abroad to the Tibetan autonomous government on exile and to the Kalon Tripa. The Dalai Lama concentrated on visiting countries where he could lead Buddhist initiations and teachings. Thus, his role as spiritual leader became clearer, a role that within this work has been labelled as a peacekeeper. Violence and tensions between human beings come out of an absence of compassion and understanding of the other's point of view. As

I have outlined within this chapter such understanding of peace and understanding requires a responsibility that the Dalai Lama has stressed as universal, including all human beings, regardless of their faith or no faith. Thus, in the following chapter I will explore such narrative of universal responsibility, or from Tibet to the world, firmly based on Tibetan Buddhism, and firmly based on the charm of a Tibetan monk who has managed to influence many by encountering them. Dialogues about science, philosophy, and our human universal responsibility have dominated the Dalai Lama's past thirty years of engagement with the world, from the moment of acceptance of the Nobel Prize for Peace in 1989, and they will be examined in the next part of this work.

Notes

1 Dalai Lamas rarely ventured outside Lhasa while the 14th Dalai Lama had travelled to attend meetings with Mao Tse-Tung in Beijing. The Fifth Dalai Lama was the one that spent more time away from Tibet in his military campaign that led him to meet the Chinese emperor, see Mario I. Aguilar, 'Ngawang Lopsang Gyatso, *chösi nyitrel*, and the Unification of Tibet in 1642', *The Tibet Journal* XLI/2, 2016, pp. 3–20.

2 Subhash C. Kashyap (ed.), 'Introduction', *The Political Philosophy of the Dalai Lama: Selected Speeches and Writings.* New Delhi: Rupa, 2014, pp. xix–xxv.

3 Michael Harris Goodman in his biography of the 14th Dalai Lama narrates the same events that took place on 17 March 1959; however, he omits any narration of a ritual moment related to the Nechung Oracle and recalls that at 4:00 p.m. two mortar shells landed at the Dalai Lama's headquarters, He cites the Dalai Lama as saying 'the first thought on the minds of every official was that I must leave the city at once'; see Michael Harris Goodman, *The Last Dalai Lama: A Biography.* London: Sidwick & Jackson, 1986, p. 299.

4 The Dalai Lama, *Freedom in Exile: The Autobiography of His Holiness the Dalai Lama of Tibet.* London: Hodder & Stoughton, 1990, p. 148.

5 The Dalai Lama, *Freedom in Exile*, p. 149.

6 Thomas Laird, *The Story of Tibet: Conversations with the Dalai Lama.* London: Atlantic Books, 2007, p. 5.

7 Robert B. Ekvall, *Religious Observances in Tibet: Patterns and Function.* Chicago, IL and London: University of Chicago Press, 1964, p. 90.

8   See Robert Ford, *Captured in Tibet*. London: George G. Harrap, 1957.
9   Ford, *Captured in Tibet*, pp. 237–238.
10 Ford, *Captured in Tibet*, p. 139.
11 This understanding of a 'liberation' from foreign powers continues being present in the Chinese contemporary literature. For example, Jiawei and Gyaincain wrote in the late 1990s:

>   At the time of the founding of the People's Republic of China (PRC) in 1949, foreign imperialist and expansionist forces incited Tibetan separatists to speed up efforts towards bringing about 'Tibetan independence' in an attempt to make impossible the liberation of Tibet,

See Wang Jiawei and Nyima Gyaincain, *The Historical Status of China's Tibet*. Beijing: China Intercontinental Press, 1997, p. 3.
12 Those who signed on behalf of the Chinese People's Government were Chief Delegate Li Wei-Han (Chairman of the Commission of Nationalities Affairs), Delegates Chang Ching-Wu, Chang Kuo-Hua, and Sun Chih-Yuan. Delegates of the local government of Tibet were Chief Delegate Kaloon Ngabou Ngawang Jigme (Ngabo Shape), Delegates Dazasak Khemey Sonam Wangdi, Khentrung Thupten Tenthar, Khenchung Thupten Lekmuun, and Rimshi Samposey Tenzin Thundup.
13 Full text available in H.E. Richardson, *Tibet and Its History*. London: Oxford University Press, 1962, Appendix 18, pp. 275–278.
14 Melvyn C. Goldstein, 'A Study of the Ldab Ldob', *Central Asiatic Journal* 9/2, 1964, pp. 125–141.
15 The 14th Dalai Lama recalled that 'one day I was in front of Lama Tsongkhapa's tomb in Ganden, during my free time. I was not there for any special sort of ritual or ceremony. I was alone and I made some prostrations in front of his tomb. I felt so moved, I felt like crying. It was some sort of special feeling', in Thomas Laird, *The Story of Tibet*, p. 126.
16 Laird, *The Story of Tibet*, p. 126.
17 Laird, *The Story of Tibet*, p. 126.
18 Laird, *The Story of Tibet*, p. 126.
19 Melvyn C. Goldstein, *A History of Modern Tibet 1913–1951: The Demise of the Lamaist State*. Berkeley: University of California Press, 1992, p. 5, note 13.
20 HH the 14th Dalai Lama, 'Preservation of Tibet's Unique Spiritual Heritage: Statement on the 40th Anniversary of the Tibetan National Uprising', Dharamshala, 10 March 1999, in Kashyap (ed). *The Political Philosophy of the Dalai Lama*, pp. 369–374.
21 Kashyap, ed., *The Political Philosophy*, p. 370.
22 Kashyap, ed., *The Political Philosophy*, p. 371.

23 Kashyap, ed., *The Political Philosophy*, p. 371.
24 Chi Wang, *The United States and China since World War II: A Brief History*. Armonk, NY: M.E. Sharpe Inc., 2013.
25 Ramon H. Myers, Michel C. Oksenberg, and David Shambaugh, eds., *Making China Policy: Lessons from the Bush and Clinton Administrations*. Lanham, MD: Rowman & Littlefield, 2001.
26 Embassy of the People's Republic of China in the United States of America, 'Jian, Clinton Hold Talks', at http://www.china-embassy.org/eng/zmgx/zysj/kldfh/t36238.htm, and the 14th Dalai Lama in Kashyap (ed). *The Political Philosophy*, pp. 371, 373.
27 HH the 14th Dalai Lama, 'A Century of Peace and Dialogue: Statement on the 41st Anniversary of the Tibetan National Uprising', Dharamshala, 10 March 2000, in Kashyap (ed). *The Political Philosophy*, pp. 375–379 at p. 376.
28 He recorded the expulsion of 1,432 monks and nuns from their monasteries and nunneries for opposing to denounce Tibetan freedom or denounce the Dalai Lama, Kashyap (ed). *The Political Philosophy*, p. 376.
29 Kashyap, ed., *The Political Philosophy*, p. 376.
30 Kashyap, ed., *The Political Philosophy*, pp. 378, 379.
31 Kashyap, ed., *The Political Philosophy*, pp. 378–379.
32 For many Tibetan commentators the person of the Dalai Lama does not provide a solution, as Chinese and Tibetans need to work together but the solution to the tensions is Tibetan organizing, see Tsering Woeser and Wang Lixiong, 'Old Lhasa Politized', *Voices from Tibet: Selected Essays and Reportage*. Honolulu, HI: University of Hawaii Press, 2014.
33 HH the Dalai Lama, 'China is Transforming: Statement on the 42nd Anniversary of the Tibetan National Uprising', Dharamshala, 10 March 2001, in Kashyap (ed), *The Political Philosophy*, pp. 380–384 at p. 381.
34 Kashyap (ed), *The Political Philosophy*, p. 381.
35 HH the Dalai Lama, 'Modernizing the Tibetan Political System: Message to the Tibetan Parliament in Exile', Dharamshala, 14 March 2011, in Kashyap (ed). *The Political Philosophy*, pp. 126–130 at p. 127.
36 Kashyap (ed), *The Political Philosophy*, pp. 127–128.
37 Kashyap (ed), *The Political Philosophy*, p. 128.
38 Kashyap (ed), *The Political Philosophy*, p. 129.
39 HH the Dalai Lama, 'Establishment of a Democratic System: Remarks on Retirement', Dharamshala, 19 March 2011, in Kashyap (ed). *The Political Philosophy*, pp. 131–135.
40 Kashyap (ed), *The Political Philosophy*, p. 131.
41 Kashyap (ed), *The Political Philosophy*, p. 133.
42 HH the 14th Dalai Lama, 'First Democratically Elected Leader: Swearing-In Ceremony of the Kalon Tripa Dr Lobsang Sangay',

Dharamshala, 12 August 2011, in Kashyap (ed). *The Political Philosophy*, pp. 136–138 at p. 138.

43 According to the International Campaign for Tibet, 156 Tibetans have immolated themselves from 2009 to 2019, see https://savetibet. org/tibetan-self-immolations/

44 Katarina Plank, 'Living Torches of Tibet: Religious and Political Implications of the Recent Self-Immolations', *Journal of Religion and Violence* 2013, 1/3, pp. 343–362.

45 'His Holiness the Dalai Lama Visits Okinawa', 12 November 2012 at https://www.dalailama.com/news/2012/his-holiness-the-dalai-lama-visits-okinawa

46 HH the 14th Dalai Lama, 'The Next Dalai Lama: Statement on the Issue of Reincarnation', Dharamshala, 14 September 2011, in Kashyap (ed). *The Political Philosophy*, pp. 139–150.

47 Kashyap (ed), *The Political Philosophy*, p. 140.

48 Kashyap (ed), *The Political Philosophy*, p. 143.

49 Kashyap (ed), *The Political Philosophy*, p. 143.

50 Kashyap (ed), *The Political Philosophy*, p. 144.

51 Kashyap (ed), *The Political Philosophy*, p. 144.

52 Kashyap (ed), *The Political Philosophy*, p. 148.

53 Kashyap (ed), *The Political Philosophy*, p. 149.

54 'The Next Incarnation of the Dalai Lama', in Kashyap (ed). *The Political Philosophy*, p. 149.

55 Kashyap (ed), *The Political Philosophy*, p. 150.

4

TOWARDS UNIVERSAL
RESPONSIBILITY

As in the case of most religious and political leaders, the Dalai Lama underwent a personal transformation on issues regarding the importance of the Tibetan presence and his own influence in a globalised community. His sense of non-violence, which he had learned from his own Tibetan Buddhist masters and that he had studied within the writings of his predecessors, was developed much later under the experience of exile.[1] The Dalai Lama experienced the inability of influencing the international community to save Tibet from a cultural genocide by China, and over the years some governments have found difficulties on their support for Tibet because of their relations with China. The People's Republic of China has exercised undue pressure on states around the world not to receive the Dalai Lama and on business cooperation without accountability on human rights issues.[2] The Dalai Lama's formation and his clear sense of compassion for all sentient beings, including the Chinese, has aided in these matters. After all the Dalai Lama has always defined his identity as that of a Buddhist monk, coming from a country where the three main monasteries had thousands of monks and where history and politics were guided by Buddhist principles of peace and interdependence. It is remarkable that his experience of exile let him develop his sense of peacebuilding and universal responsibility without any distractions or change of direction.

I have outlined so far the foundations for the Dalai Lama's attitudes within his monastic formation, the dharma, and particularly the *lam rim chen mo* and the *Bodhicharyāvatāra*, as well as his personal and first-hand experience of exile and of listening to the testimonies of many Tibetans who have experienced the destruction of Tibetan ways of life and values under Chinese occupation. From 1959 until the conferring of the Nobel Prize in 1989 the Dalai Lama cared deeply and single-mindedly for the Tibetans and their cultural survival in India. This was his main task and given the lack of Internet and global communications he relied on friends and associates that helped him not only to keep the memory of Tibet alive in the world but also within India. It was the government of Nehru that had secured his safety and had given lands and financing for schools, hospitals, and housing for the Tibetan community in India. It is in this period also that Tibetan monks were central to the arrival of Buddhism in Europe and North America and the development of a connection between Tibetan Buddhism and other religious communities in the West, particularly the majority Christian churches at that time. One must understand that the Dalai Lama was young and inexperienced in global affairs as before his exile Tibet had remained isolated and only in contact with British colonial officers stationed in India and Chinese envoys stationed in Lhasa. I would argue that the 'coming out' of a global peacebuilding and a universal responsibility was first manifested in the Dalai Lama's Nobel Prize Lecture in December 1989 in Oslo, Norway. Tibet and the Tibetans were at the centre of his concerns, but it was a central occasion for his message to the world stating that Tibet and the Dalai Lama had a lot to offer to the development of a shared world and its values for the future.

The Nobel Prize and the peacebuilding agenda

The Nobel Prize Committee expressed its clear sense that the Nobel Prize was awarded to the Dalai Lama because he exercised leadership since 1959 in a non-violent manner.[3] It would have been easier for the Dalai Lama to arrange for a foreign guerrilla army to liberate parts of Tibet. In a sense the Khampa warriors were that fighting army with the help of the CIA until 1969, and then they continued their fight on their own until 1974 when the Nepalese Army was sent to capture them. The Dalai Lama sent them a tape ordering to surrender as to be spared. Some of them killed themselves and others ended up in Nepal rather than in China. They did not want to remain in their home territories because in Nepal they could practice their religion. With these twenty years between the end of the CIA support of the Khampa warriors and the Nobel Lecture, it can be argued that the young Dalai Lama realized that force against the Chinese would not work, and that violence would only bring further repression towards Tibetans within China. But this was not a political decision, but a decision that relied on compassion and for a globalized humanity beyond Tibet.

During the Nobel Lecture the Dalai Lama set the foundations for what was to be his contribution and the contribution of the Tibetan people to universal responsibility.[4] In the insightful comments by Jane Robinett, the Dalai Lama fulfilled the role of other public intellectuals and other exiles as well as the role of other public intellectuals, following the tradition of non-violent rhetoric practised by Mahatma Gandhi and Martin Luther King.[5] In the opening of the lecture the Dalai Lama thanked many friends and new friends for attending the occasion and he told them:

> I meet people in different parts of the world, I am always reminded that we are all basically alike. We are all human beings. Maybe we wore different clothes, our skin is of a different colour, or we speak different languages. That is on the surface. But basically, we are the same human beings.[6]

Further, he spoke about the necessity to learn to live in peace with each other and with nature because we all live in the same small planet.[7] Interdependency between communities remained the strong message from the Dalai Lama who defined himself as 'a simple monk'.[8] The Nobel Prize, according to the Dalai Lama, was merited by Tibetans because they had endured forty years of foreign occupation. However, he made very clear that he didn't have a feeling of anger towards the occupiers, responsible for destruction and suffering; the occupiers, according to the Dalai Lama, are 'human beings who struggle to find happiness and deserve our compassion'.[9]

For the principle of interdependence, the karmic laws of Buddhism were time and again invoked by the Dalai Lama in his lecture as to set in front of a global audience the principle of universal responsibility not only for human beings but also for nature itself. The following paragraph summarises such deep-seated Buddhist doctrine brought to contemporary life by the Dalai Lama:

> The realization that we are all basically the same, human beings, who seek happiness and try to avoid suffering, is very helpful in developing a sense of brotherhood and sisterhood; a warm feeling of love and compassion for others. This, in turn, is essential.

Within such shared humanity we are all interdependent, and 'as interdependent, we have no other choice than to develop what I call a sense of universal responsibility'.[10] In a global family, continues the Dalai Lama, we are happy when there is peace between warring factions. Within such understanding the reality is that all human phenomena are interrelated. Peace is not only the absence of war, but it can only be meaningful to all human beings where human rights are respected, where people are fed, and where individuals and nations are free.[11] In order to create such peace, material and spiritual development are needed.[12] Both go together, and Tibetans can offer their practice of inner peace whereby they have articulated a life in which material development also needs inner peace. Feelings of love and kindness are central to such inner peace and they can be developed through religious practice and also through non-religious practices.[13] The important attitude and practice is that we take our responsibility for each other and for nature seriously.[14] However, universal responsibility does not relate only to the geographical but to the different issues that we face in our planet. Universal responsibility does not bring the responsibility to the state first but in a Buddhist manner to the individual whereby inner peace at the individual level is needed in order to contribute to the peace of a community, and then to other community, and communities, and finally to the state.[15]

It is a fact that Tibetans are known for their peacefulness and the Dalai Lama paid tribute to whom he called 'his mentor', i.e. Mahatma Gandhi.[16] Indeed, the Nobel Lecture was preceded by the Dalai Lama's acceptance speech on 10 September 1989.[17] In that speech he recognised that he tried to follow the teachings of the Buddha and the great sages of India and Tibet, and that the Nobel Committee's recognition was not to him but to his practice of the true value of altruism, love, compassion, and non-violence.[18] The Dalai Lama accepted the prize in tribute not only to the oppressed and those who worked for world peace but as a tribute to Mahatma Gandhi whose life taught and inspired him. He also accepted the prize in the name of six million Tibetans who would liberate Tibet with truth, courage, and determination as their weapons. He repeated the same universal description that 'we are all basically the same human beings.'[19] Violence can only breed more violence and suffering. As a monk, the Dalai Lama recognised that his concern was for the whole human family and for all sentient beings who suffer.[20] All suffering comes from ignorance and the Dalai Lama reiterated his call to cultivate a 'universal responsibility for one another and the planet we share'.[21]

The road to universal responsibility

In the following years the Dalai Lama proceeded to outline, express, and develop issues related to a universal responsibility in front of audiences that wanted to hear a Nobel Prize winner, particularly after the crushing of the student protestors in Tiananmen Square. The message remained sustained and clear: the sameness and unity of human beings and the responsibility of every individual to all others and to nature. Such sense of human rights and the rights of nature seemed to have been a new discovery in the 21st century, but it goes back to all religions. Thus, the emphasis by the Dalai Lama on the common search for happiness and the avoidance of suffering by all sentient beings, humans and animals, was stressed to the Congress of the International League for the Abolition of the Death Penalty in December 1993.[22] For the Dalai Lama humans and animals have agency as Buddhism believes, and they need to take the right decisions for them and for others. Human life is precious for all religions; however, within Buddhism reincarnation as a human being has a bigger responsibility and it is a difficult one.[23] Within such path to spiritual liberation human beings take the wrong decisions when they have feelings of selfishness, greed, hatred, or pride. As human beings we live together and are dependent on each other and develop codes of behaviour that are moral through philosophy or religion and that allow us to live in peace and harmony.

The Dalai Lama particularly takes the death penalty as a kind of revenge because the person is not given the chance to change, life is ended, and the punishment is final.[24] For Buddhists it is a sin to take the life of even an insect but it is a grave offence to cut a human life in which an opportunity has been given. Such action has consequences in terms of karmic law for those who have taken such life away. In the words of the Dalai Lama, 'killing offenders does not solve the problems of law'.[25] Thus, compassion and kindness through education and the establishment of a universal responsibility can improve such a situation.[26] As outlined by Mahatma Gandhi violence breeds more violence and capital punishment is a kind of violence.[27] An eye for an eye it only makes the rest of the world blind.[28]

Universal responsibility and environment

One of the new contributions by the Dalai Lama to peacekeeping and universal responsibility was the interconnection with nature, animals, and the environment. It seems that within the 21st century such connections are a given but thirty years ago they were fresh, new, and ignored outside the Indian religions. The Dalai Lama was digging in his Buddhist tradition, as I have outlined in previous chapters. Thus, for those who were not familiar with his thought and way of life he had to expand on his sense of interconnectedness between humans, animals, and their environment. He spoke already in 1994 of 'an environmental crisis that threatens our air, water and trees, along with the vast number of beautiful life forms that are the very foundation of existence on this small planet we share'.[29] In order to meet the challenges of the future, according to the Dalai Lama, human beings have to develop a greater sense of universal responsibility.[30] In his words universal responsibility is 'the best foundation for world peace, the equitable use of natural resources and, through concern for future generations, the proper care of the environment'.[31] Further, interdependence becomes the best form of self-interest.[32]

Within the Dalai Lama's aspirations of interdependence, one finds religions as source of service and demilitarisation as a goal in order to free human resources 'for protection of the environment, relief of poverty, and sustainable human development'.[33] Further, human rights constitute parameters of universal responsibility because we have all been born as part of one great human family.[34] And at the beginning of the new millennium the Dalai Lama reiterated the need for an internal and external disarmament.[35] Internal disarmament requires the end of negative emotions that lead to violence and external disarmament requires the end of nuclear weapons with a total demilitarisation throughout the world.[36] The end of military areas had been, one must remember, a master plan by the Dalai Lama, already mentioned for Tibet during his Nobel Prize speech and a subject to which he returned many times. For an end to any military presence in Tibet would have secured a cultural survival and a heaven of spiritual and natural conservation for all Tibetans. The Chinese never responded to such proposal, but the absence of armies throughout the world was a solution to inhumanity to which the Dalai Lama returned time and again with the authority of someone who was not leading an army any longer. Another topic that he addressed as part of a universal responsibility for the new millennium was the gap between the rich and the poor whereby some had too many resources while others starved to death.[37] The care of the environment was another topic that the Dalai Lama addressed as central for a universal responsibility, particularly the fact that most rivers in Southeast Asia flow from Tibet, and therefore the care of the Tibetan environment impacted several other regions.

For the Dalai Lama non-violence has been central to such universal responsibility and he spoke clearly on the first anniversary of 9/11.[38] While he condemned and regretted the violent events of 9/11 he suggested that retaliation after those events would not be the best solution. He suggested using non-violence as a measure against terrorism as a long-term strategy. Non-violence provides the solution to misunderstandings, which are common and expected within an international fora of nations.[39] Education is the solution for creating an interdependence that learns that violence is counterproductive.[40] However, it seems that those who were aware of the Dalai Lama's thoughts and wishes did not listen a few years later when the armies of the United States and allies retaliated against terrorist groups that were present in states and territories of the Middle East.

The Dalai Lama used his public meetings with large amounts of people and his supporters to elaborate further thoughts on peace and universal responsibility, and indeed he influenced the reflections on human responsibility of many. Thus, in London in 2008 and speaking to the Tibet Society, the Dalai Lama recognised that he had three main commitments until his death: the promotion of human values, the promotion of religious harmony, and naturally the cause of Tibet.[41] These three principles became in the words of Sophia Stril-Rever's work the Dalai Lama's spiritual biography in which the change can be seen between the boy-monk to the fully developed spiritual master in Tibetan Buddhism, a Dalai Lama.[42] Speaking to the Tibet Society the Dalai Lama spoke of a self-evaluation, of being a semi-retired advisor to the Tibetan government, of living in democracy and therefore sometimes being ignored.[43] However, this was one of the few occasions in which he expanded on the purpose of his visits to different countries. During those visits the Dalai Lama confided that he tried to address two issues, which he considered central to his spiritual advice to the contemporary world: the promotion of human values and the promotion of religious harmony.[44]

The Dalai Lama certainly realised that during his visits there was also a developing politization of his presence because of the ongoing situation in Tibet. I witnessed such change in his visit to London in September 2015 when the Dalai Lama on the year of his 80th birthday spoke at venues such as the O2 Arena. Not only the usual Chinese protestors were organised by the police at the entrance to the O2 Arena but very vociferous protestors belonging to the Buddhist Shugden community, the new Kadampa tradition in the UK, organised a name and shame protest, interfering with individuals like me who wanted to listen to and to make His Holiness very welcome.[45] They were noisy and forceful in their protest. The Shugden controversy posed questions in Europe about the unity of Tibetans and their neutral contribution to society's spiritual values because of such protests. Years before the Dalai Lama had forbidden the spiritual connections with Shugden, and even in 2000 the High Court of India had to deal with a criminal accusation of psychological torture against the Dalai Lama by members of the Tibetan community, due to his condemnation of Shugden.[46] Shugden, for believers, is a protective deity, even a fully enlightened form of Manjushri; for others he is a dangerous spirit known as Gyel-po with no place in Tibetan Buddhism and rightly condemned by the Dalai Lama. This controversy goes back to the Fifth Dalai Lama who led part of Deprung monastery while another monk Sonam Drakba Gyaltsen led another part of the monastery. In 1650 Drakba Gyaltsen died and there were accusations of poisoning by the Fifth Dalai Lama.[47] Those were denied at that time; however, those who supported the accusations against the Fifth Dalai Lama suggested that Drakba Gyaltsen had reincarnated in the spirit Gyel-po. It is important to explore the Dalai Lama's calls for inner peace and universal responsibility amid these religious controversies simply because the Dalai Lama has tried to speak to the followers of Shugden but without much result. They are relentless in their public accusations against the Dalai Lama, and I have been the recipient of numerous envelopes containing documents and texts that support their case, asking me as a Buddhist scholar to reject the claims and condemn the 14th Dalai Lama's stand on Shugden.

In my opinion, and as I will explore further in the last section of this work, the Dalai Lama has spoken of universal and global responsibility in all his talks to non-Tibetan audiences since 1973 and has been a peacekeeper within the public protests of the followers of Shugden and the pro-China lobby.[48] The Dalai Lama considers that the same desires for happiness are present in all human beings, in particular at a very basic level, a desire for a pleasant day. However, problems arise because a human being decides to think only about his own wishes and forgets to include and think of others. All human desires are interconnected as we are part of a large human family of six billion people.[49] The Dalai Lama has many times returned to the Buddhist concept of considering all sentient beings as the mother to whom you should be as close as your own mother, finding a sympathetic audience within Hindus because of their appreciation of the sacred river Ganges as 'mother'.[50] Other religions have suggested that all creation is created by God, including other sentient beings and the whole world.[51] How do we develop a sense of global responsibility within such differences? For the Dalai Lama peace and inner satisfaction comes from a mental attitude, not from resources or state policies.[52] Such inner satisfaction and mental attitude starts with human affection as a basic instinct from a mother to her child.[53] Thus, affection and compassion are at the centre of such mental attitude towards others.[54] The Dalai Lama mentioned a monk that had been many years in a Chinese prison and who in a visit to Dharamshala was asked by the Dalai Lama if he had faced danger many times. He answered that in a couple of occasions he faced the danger of not feeling compassion for the Chinese, and that those moments were very dangerous indeed.[55] Those attitudes of compassion create inner peace and they create world peace because they show ways of compassion without anger, anger which creates violence and war in the world.[56] As the Dalai Lama had outlined previously, 'inner disarmament' brings inner peace and a lasting outer disarmament in the world. Tensions between human beings will happen but dialogue as the effort to understand the other's point of view will create that possibility of peace between those who can even disagree on their opinions. There are many religions and they must be respected, as I respect somebody else's religion; there is one truth in my religion but there are also several truths when one examines the realities in which human beings live.[57]

Towards a global responsibility

Time and again the Dalai Lama returns to the reality that 'we are all human beings' and that we are all dependent on each other, foundation for compassion that the Dalai Lama referred to within the opening of the ceremony in which he accepted the

Templeton Foundation Award in 2012.[58] At St Paul's Cathedral in London, when accepting the Templeton Foundation Award, the Dalai Lama set the foundations of self-confidence as a process of opening the mind to actions that are truthful, honest, and sincere.[59] For self-confidence comes from that awareness that we are all human beings who develop an atmosphere of trust reducing fear, anxiety, and loneliness regardless of whether you are a believer or not.[60] Such inner value gives the potential and the daily opportunities to interact with others, opportunities that finally money does not give.[61] In the case of the world religions, these religions are portrayed as traditions that provide divisions and this should not be the case because all religions speak of forgiveness based on love and compassion.[62] Indeed, in Jane Compson's thoughtful analysis of the Dalai Lama's position vis-à-vis the world religions, she concludes that 'what at first sight might seem like simply a theory of religions can be seen as one facet of the Dalai Lama's compassionate practice'.[63] Moreover, 'friendship comes from such love and compassion, from friendship comes cooperation and global responsibility'.[64] The Dalai Lama describes the 20th century as a century of war and he argues for the thinking of one world and the oneness of humanity.[65]

Love and compassion become a central motto for such interconnectedness and universal responsibility. However, the Dalai Lama continued outlining the characteristics and wishes for his life as a monk by, one would say, demythologising religion in general and Tibetan Buddhism in particular. As a Tibetan monk, he spoke many times as if teaching his audience sitting in the position of an eastern teacher rather than standing with a script in the position of a western teacher. In one of those occasions he taught on compassion and the individual and asked, 'what is the purpose of life?'[66] For him, a shared desire is to be happy. But how to achieve such happiness? He argued that happiness and suffering can be divided into two categories: mental and physical.[67] Of the two categories the mind is the one that acquires more importance, and therefore one should devote continuous efforts to bring about mental peace.[68] The Dalai Lama's experience regarding mental peace is clear: 'I have found that the greatest degree of inner tranquillity comes from the development of love and compassion'.[69] Thus, by becoming closer to others one puts the mind at ease.[70] The need for love from the time that we are born is essential so that material things do not provide such love, and they do not satisfy our need for love 'because our deeper identity and true character lie in the subjective nature of the mind'.[71] Love is followed by an ongoing compassion so that love does not become a selfish attachment. For the Dalai Lama, 'true compassion is not just an emotional response, but a firm commitment founded on reason'.[72] Thus, a compassionate attitude does not change when others behave negatively. The development of compassion is not easy, but it can be done, particularly by eliminating such individual existence without the existence of others.

Is global responsibility comparable to a universal responsibility? I would argue that these are interchangeable concepts in the Dalai Lama's language, based on actions of compassion. However, for listeners and those who attend events and read books about the Dalai Lama, such concepts have a slightly different meaning because their understanding and subsequent actions have a slightly different meaning within Buddhist and non-Buddhist actions. Thus, when the Dalai Lama addresses audiences that are not Buddhist the slightly different meaning is understood in the context of two different settings. For a Tibetan Buddhist compassion arises out of the training of the mind but extends to all sentient beings, that is humans, animals, and the whole of creation, including plants. Universal responsibility then for a Buddhist covers compassion for the whole of creation not because it arises out of survival or because the planet can be diminished with disastrous consequences for humans, i.e. the ecological utilitarian argument. Instead, in Tibetan Buddhism compassion embraces all creations. However, when the argument of compassion relates to non-Buddhist audiences the concept of a global responsibility, which in the Dalai Lama's act of speech means universal, becomes care for humans in the first place, and sometimes the care for the rest of creation.

It is crucial at this stage to return to the text of Shantideva's *Bodhicharyāvatāra* chapter 9 and the cultivation of wisdom. We have so far engaged with the Dalai Lama's actions towards peace and non-violence and within such teachings the Dalai Lama has answered important points on how to train the mind towards compassion and how to engage with human beings. However, Shantideva's text provides a further insight that is central to the life and actions of the Dalai Lama: wisdom. For Shantideva's *Bodhicharyāvatāra* relates wisdom as the attainment of enlightenment, and according to the Dalai Lama 'all aspects of the teachings of the Buddha are intended to lead individuals to the state of full enlightenment'.[73] For the beginning of chapter 9 sets the summary of all teachings:

> All these branches of the Doctrine
> The Enlightened Sage expounded for the sake of wisdom.
> Therefore they must cultivate this wisdom
> Who wish to have an end of suffering.

> (*Bodhicharyāvatāra* 9.1)

Chapter 9 of the *Bodhicharyāvatāra* is a very complex chapter in that Shantideva's teaching of this chapter was done with an audience at Nalanda and the audience to this chapter was already versed in the teachings and the texts associated with the teachings of the Buddha. Thus, in the commentary and translation of the *Bodhicharyāvatāra* by the Padmakara Translation Group the note on this verse suggests that 'this chapter was no doubt intended as a brilliant and perhaps even light-hearted exposition of a highly recondite subject to a specialist audience of philosophers and academics'.[74] It is this very point that provides an important marker of semantic understanding when it comes to the Dalai Lama's teaching and addresses to audiences throughout the world. It has been customary that the Dalai Lama when visiting a place addresses a very large audience of supporters and those who want to listen to his understanding of life but at the same time has other activities such as initiations or conferring of Buddhist blessings in which his message of compassion, peace, and responsibility changes language from global to universal, from compassion to love, from enlightenment to wisdom as it was the case of Shantideva's teaching in chapter 9 of the *Bodhicharyāvatāra*. Such distinctions are important in order to understand his role as peacekeeper, particularly within his visits to Europe and North America, places in which his audiences are less able to listen to Buddhist teaching and the wisdom of the Dalai Lama. They live lives within the global rather than the universal and they want to know what to do with actions executed quickly rather than following the Dalai Lama's universality of mind and the training of the mind.

While in this chapter I have explored the thought processes of compassion by the Dalai Lama since the conferring of the Nobel Prize for Peace in 1989, in the following chapter I will explore the meeting of the Dalai Lama with audiences, scientists, and personalities in Europe and North America with the Dalai Lama's intention of fostering non-violence, peace, and a fuller understanding of a shared humanity.

Notes

1 His Holiness the Dalai Lama, *The Path to Freedom: Freedom in Exile and Ancient Wisdom, Modern World*. London: Abacus, 2005.

2 For example, when I was leading a major research project on the history of Tibet the university where I conducted such research was pressurised to remove from our webpage the letter of support that the Dalai Lama had kindly sent to us. By not having much publicity the research project was a successful one, and the university authorities had a difficult balancing act between the pressure by Chinese students and the fact that the Dalai Lama is part of the university having received an honorary doctorate in 1996. This has been the experience of all Scottish universities.

3 'A Buddhist Advocate for Peace and Freedom' at https://www.nobelprize.org/prizes/peace/1989/lama/facts/

4 HH the 14th Dalai Lama, 'Power of Truth and Non-Violence: Nobel Lecture', 11 December 1989, in Subhash C. Kashyap, *The Political Philosophy of the Dalai Lama: Selected Speeches and Writings*. New Delhi: Rupa, 2014, pp. 156–165.

5 Jane Robinett, 'A Rhetoric of Non-Violence: The Dalai Lama's 1989 Nobel Peace Prize Lecture: A Rhetoric of Non-Violence', *Advances in the History of Rhetoric* 18, Supplement 1, 2015, pp. S227–S244.

6 Kashyap, *The Political Philosophy of the Dalai Lama*, p. 156.

7 Kashyap, *The Political Philosophy of the Dalai Lama*, p. 156.

8 Kashyap, *The Political Philosophy of the Dalai Lama*, pp. 156, 160 cf. 153 in HH the XIV Dalai Lama, 'Tribute to Mahatma Gandhi: Nobel Peace Prize Acceptance Speech', University of Aula, Oslo, 10 December 1989.

9   Kashyap, *The Political Philosophy of the Dalai Lama*, p. 157.
10 Kashyap, *The Political Philosophy of the Dalai Lama*, p. 157.
11 Kashyap, *The Political Philosophy of the Dalai Lama*, p. 158.
12 The Dalai Lama recognised that in the past material development in Tibet was not as important as spiritual development; according to him that was a mistake, see Kashyap, *The Political Philosophy of the Dalai Lama*, p. 158.
13 Kashyap, *The Political Philosophy of the Dalai Lama*, p. 159.
14 Kashyap, *The Political Philosophy of the Dalai Lama*, p. 159.
15 Kashyap, *The Political Philosophy of the Dalai Lama*, p. 159.
16 Kashyap, *The Political Philosophy of the Dalai Lama*, p. 160.
17 HH the 14th Dalai Lama, 'Tribute to Mahatma Gandhi: Nobel Peace Prize Acceptance Speech', University of Aula, Oslo, 10 December 1989, in Kashyap, *The Political Philosophy of the Dalai Lama*, pp. 153–155.
18 Kashyap, *The Political Philosophy of the Dalai Lama*, p. 153.
19 Kashyap, *The Political Philosophy of the Dalai Lama*, p. 153.
20 Kashyap, *The Political Philosophy of the Dalai Lama*, p. 155.
21 Kashyap, *The Political Philosophy of the Dalai Lama*, p. 155.
22 HH the 14th Dalai Lama, 'Violence to Violence: Address to the Congress of the International League for the Abolition of Death Penalty', European Parliament, Brussels, 9–10 December 1933, in Kashyap, *The Political Philosophy of the Dalai Lama*, pp. 431–433 at p. 431.
23 Kashyap, *The Political Philosophy of the Dalai Lama*, p. 431.
24 Kashyap, *The Political Philosophy of the Dalai Lama*, p. 432.
25 Kashyap, *The Political Philosophy of the Dalai Lama*, p. 432.
26 Kashyap, *The Political Philosophy of the Dalai Lama*, pp. 432–433.
27 Kashyap, *The Political Philosophy of the Dalai Lama*, p. 433.
28 For recent works on Gandhi see Talat Ahmed, *Mohandas Gandhi: Experiments in Civil Disobedience*. London: Pluto Press, 2019, and the forthcoming work by Ramin Jahanbegloo in the Routledge and CRC Press Series Peacemakers.
29 HH the 14th Dalai Lama, 'Universal Responsibility and Environment: Speech at the Society for Protection of Nature, Israel', 22 March 1994, in Kashyap, *The Political Philosophy of the Dalai Lama*, pp. 434–438 at p. 434.
30 Kashyap, *The Political Philosophy of the Dalai Lama*, p. 434.
31 Kashyap, *The Political Philosophy of the Dalai Lama*, p. 434.
32 Kashyap, *The Political Philosophy of the Dalai Lama*, p. 435.
33 Kashyap, *The Political Philosophy of the Dalai Lama*, p. 436.
34 HH the XIV Dalai Lama, 'Universal Responsibility as Key to Human Survival and Progress: Message on the 50th Anniversary of the Universal Declaration of Human Rights', Dharamshala, 7 December 1998, in Kashyap, *The Political Philosophy of the Dalai Lama*, pp. 439–440 at p. 439.

35 HH the XIV Dalai Lama, 'Century of Dialogue and Discussion: Message for the New Millennium', 1 January 2000 in Kashyap, *The Political Philosophy of the Dalai Lama*, pp. 441–442.

36 Kashyap, *The Political Philosophy of the Dalai Lama*, p. 442.

37 Kashyap, *The Political Philosophy of the Dalai Lama*, p. 442.

38 HH the XIV Dalai Lama, 'Non-Violence to Control Terrorism: Message on the Commemoration of the 1st Anniversary of 11 September 2001', 1 September 2002, in Kashyap, *The Political Philosophy of the Dalai Lama*, pp. 443–445.

39 Kashyap, *The Political Philosophy of the Dalai Lama*, p. 444.

40 Kashyap, *The Political Philosophy of the Dalai Lama*, p. 445.

41 HH the XIV Dalai Lama, 'Universal Responsibility in the Modern World', Royal Albert Hall, London, 22 May 2008 in Kashyap, *The Political Philosophy of the Dalai Lama*, pp. 446–458 at p. 447.

42 While the Dalai Lama spoke at the Royal Albert Hall in May 2008, he had approved the term 'spiritual' to his understanding of this universal responsibility of interconnectedness. Sophia Stril-Rever had articulated these connections within her work in French that later was translated into English, see *His Holiness the Dalai Lama, My Spiritual Autobiography*. London: Rider, 2010.

43 Kashyap, *The Political Philosophy of the Dalai Lama*, p. 448.

44 Kashyap, *The Political Philosophy of the Dalai Lama*, p. 448.

45 '"Extremist" Sect Threatens Protest against the Dalai Lama during UK Visit', *The Guardian* 13 June 2015 at https://www.theguardian.com/world/2015/jun/13/dalai-lama-uk-visit-extremist-protests Accessed 01 May 2020.

46 Directions India High Court New Delhi 18 December 2000 in R.P. Mitra, 'Politics of Religion: The Worship of Shugden among the Tibetans', *Indian Anthropologist* 2002/2, 1&2, pp. 47–58.

47 G. Dreyfus, 'The Shukden Affair: History and Nature of a Quarrel', *Journal of the International Association of Buddhist Studies* 22/1–2, University of Lausanne.

48 Kashyap, *The Political Philosophy of the Dalai Lama*, p. 448.

49 Kashyap, *The Political Philosophy of the Dalai Lama*, p. 448.

50 Kashyap, *The Political Philosophy of the Dalai Lama*, p. 448.

51 Kashyap, *The Political Philosophy of the Dalai Lama*, p. 449.

52 Kashyap, *The Political Philosophy of the Dalai Lama*, p. 450.

53 Kashyap, *The Political Philosophy of the Dalai Lama*, pp. 450–451.

54 Kashyap, *The Political Philosophy of the Dalai Lama*, p. 451.

55 Kashyap, *The Political Philosophy of the Dalai Lama*, p. 452.

56 Kashyap, *The Political Philosophy of the Dalai Lama*, p. 454.

57 Kashyap, *The Political Philosophy of the Dalai Lama*, pp. 454–455.

58 HH the XIV Dalai Lama, 'Human Rights, Democracy and Freedom: On the 60th Anniversary of the Universal Declaration of Human Rights', Dharamshala, 10 December 2008, in Kashyap,

The Political Philosophy of the Dalai Lama, pp. 459–464 at p. 459, and 'Sense of Global Responsibility: Templeton Award Ceremony', St. Paul's Cathedral, London, 14 May 2012, in Kashyap, *The Political Philosophy of the Dalai Lama*, pp. 465–470 at p. 465.

59 Kashyap, *The Political Philosophy of the Dalai Lama*, p. 466.
60 Kashyap, *The Political Philosophy of the Dalai Lama*, p. 466.
61 Kashyap, *The Political Philosophy of the Dalai Lama*, p. 466.
62 Kashyap, *The Political Philosophy of the Dalai Lama*, p. 466.
63 Jane Compson, 'The Dalai Lama and the World Religions: A False Friend?', *Religious Studies* 32/2, June 1996, pp. 271–279 at p. 278.
64 Kashyap, *The Political Philosophy of the Dalai Lama*, p. 467.
65 Kashyap, *The Political Philosophy of the Dalai Lama*, p. 468.
66 HH the XIV Dalai Lama, 'Compassion and the Individual', Writings 1991, in Kashyap, *The Political Philosophy of the Dalai Lama*, pp. 473–482 at p. 473.
67 Kashyap, *The Political Philosophy of the Dalai Lama*, p. 473.
68 Kashyap, *The Political Philosophy of the Dalai Lama*, p. 473.
69 Kashyap, *The Political Philosophy of the Dalai Lama*, p. 473.
70 Kashyap, *The Political Philosophy of the Dalai Lama*, p. 474.
71 Kashyap, *The Political Philosophy of the Dalai Lama*, p. 477.
72 Kashyap, *The Political Philosophy of the Dalai Lama*, p. 478.
73 The Dalai Lama, *Practising Wisdom: The Perfection of Shantideva's Bodhisattva Way*. Translated and edited by Thupten Jinpa. Somerville, MA: Wisdom Publications, 2005, p. 17.
74 Shāntideva, *The Way of the Bodhisattva: A Translation of the Bodhicharyāvatāra*. Translated from the Tibetan by the Padmakara Translation Group. Boston, MA, and London: Shambala, 2006, note 106, pp. 208–209.

5

NON-VIOLENCE AND
WORLD TEACHINGS

This chapter explores the Dalai Lama as a traveller for peace, as he journeyed to many countries in order to speak at conferences, receive awards, meet presidents and prime ministers, and aid any possibilities of world peace and understanding, inspiring students and admirers. Indeed, for most people the Dalai Lama has been known to them through the global media and the reports of his visits to different countries. For some it could seem strange that a monk is not in his monastery but the conditions of the 1959 exile from Tibet have meant in practice that for most of that time in exile the Dalai Lama has not resided within a monastery but in his house in Dharamshala. He served as head of the Tibetan government in exile until 2011, and then he has continued serving as spiritual leader of Tibetan Buddhists. The world has changed and expanded to be a global community, a reality very different than when the 13th and the 14th Dalai Lamas visited Beijing in the 19th and 20th century. At that time, the world was more contained within empires, and Tibet related to close neighbours such as Mongolia, China, and British India. The containment of a globalised world happened within empires, their interests and their competition for resources, lands, influence, and religious conversions. However, with the 14th Dalai Lama's exit from Tibet and exile in India made a Tibetan world became immersed within a larger globalised world. After 1959 there was the need to request support and understanding for Tibet from European and North American countries. Years later, and particularly after the award of the 1989 Nobel Prize for Peace to the Dalai Lama, invitations to speak and to visit many countries became abundant. The aims of public speaking and meetings were clearly set by the Dalai Lama in London in 2008 when addressing the Tibet Society, and those aims related to the Dalai Lama's three main commitments until his death: the promotion of human values, the promotion of religious harmony, and naturally the cause of Tibet.[1]

Responsible citizenship and the global village

Before receiving the Nobel Prize in 1989 the Dalai Lama visited Emory University in the United States in 1987. The initial invitation came from Professor John Fenton, a professor of religion at Emory. His second visit took place in September 1995 as his first stop in a visit to four American cities over twelve days in the United States. Those who had invited the Dalai Lama celebrated his 60th birthday and he received the first Emory Presidential Medal and spoke to 4,000 people gathered at the Woodruff Physical Education Center. It was clear that the Dalai Lama felt at home at Emory University and during that second visit ideas for a collaboration between Tibetans and scientists at Emory became important. One could say that the Dalai Lama during this period wanted to influence the youth and the American students who embraced the Dalai Lama as their hero and their champion. The reception he received at several convocations in American universities was comparable to that of his own people. His third visit to Emory University was in 1998 when he delivered the commencement address on 11 May and received an Honorary Doctorate in Divinity. During that visit, the Dalai Lama's Foundation and Emory University started the Emory–Tibet Partnership (ETP) to bring together the best of Western and Tibetan intellectual traditions. The partnership was a natural development that had started when Lobsang Tenzin Negi, a Tibetan monk, entered Emory's Institute of Liberal Arts. He worked with his advisor Dr Robert A. Paul who was familiar with Western and Tibetan models of the mind, being a cultural anthropologist and a psychoanalyst. The ETP developed collaborative projects between Emory and Negi's alma mater Drepung Loseling Monastic University with the associate membership of the Library of Tibetan

Works and Archives, the Institute of Buddhist Dialectics, the Tibetan Medical Institute, and other Tibetan socio-cultural and monastic institutions based in India.

Later, on 5 February 2007 the Dalai Lama was appointed Presidential Distinguished Professor at Emory University, the first university appointment accepted by him. In his words of acceptance, the Dalai Lama expressed his belief that education is the tool for a just and peaceful society and he prepared the way for his own involvement at Emory University by stating that 'I have long believed in and advocated a dialogue and cross-fertilization between science and spirituality, as both are essential for enriching human life and alleviating suffering on both individual and global levels'.[2] Through that formal and institutional appointment students and staff from Emory University started a yearly study-trip-abroad in Dharamshala, which was a great opportunity for staff and students to attend the Dalai Lama's teachings. Emory University started a programme of scholarships for Tibetan students studying at Emory.

Further visits by the Dalai Lama to Emory took place in 2010 and 2013. A landmark of the cooperation between the Dalai Lama's Foundation and Emory University was the foundation of the Center for Contemplative Science and Compassion-Based Ethics.[3] The center has carried out extensive work on the relation between the hard sciences and Tibetan foundational understandings of the mind, neuroscience, physics, and biology. An important part of such cooperation has been the Emory–Tibet Science Initiative as a programme of education for Tibetan monks and nuns in modern science and the production of textbooks by Emory scholars on neuroscience, biology, and physics. Every year sixteen Emory science staff travelled to Dharamshala to offer a six-week summer course to ninety Tibetan monks and nuns who then became 'leaders in the convergence of science and spirituality'.[4] Every year Emory hosted an international conference on science translation in order to expand a Tibetan lexicon on science, defining and standardising terminology and concepts. Further, meditation research scholars at Emory offered contemplative programmes for educating the Heart and Mind in schools and hospitals with an emphasis on underserved populations in Atlanta. Recently, the Dalai Lama had to post-pone his 2017 visit to Emory due to exhaustion.[5]

During his 2013 visit the Dalai Lama argued for the possi-bility of uniting religious and secular principles in a collective set of morals, which he called 'secular ethics'.[6] Such interesting proposal was developed within a conversation the Dalai Lama had with a group of Emory academic staff after the Director for the Center for Ethics and Professor of Bioethics Paul Wolfe summarised for the participants the Dalai Lama's book *Beyond Religion: Ethics for a Whole World* in which the Dalai Lama discussed morality through the Buddhist ideas of compassion and discernment.[7] In the general discussion and as part of a lec-ture and discussion series, the Dalai Lama added motivation to behaviour and argued for the testing of scripture and doctrine together with personal experience and evidence. For within the concept of universal responsibility and the general aspects of compassion, and within the North American context, the Dalai Lama started developing the inculturation of Buddhist concepts within the context of democratic values and the conversations about non-violence and ethical war of retaliation after 9/11. The unity of the programme for the Dalai Lama's visit was found through the possible unity and dialogue between two worlds: the Tibetan and the science-based contemporary Western thought.[8]

The influence of the Dalai Lama on thinking and educational processes in U.S. universities became significant within a climate in which China did not have the influence that it would have later. Such influence and opening by the U.S. universities had come to the forefront after the Dalai Lama received the U.S. Congres-sional Medal on 17 October 2007 from U.S. President George W. Bush at Capitol Hill in Washington D.C. In his acceptance speech the Dalai Lama remembered his own education by his mother and the whole Buddhist tradition in Lhasa that taught him to be kind, honest, and caring while understanding interde-pendence and human potential for infinite compassion.[9] In his speech, the Dalai Lama emphasised the importance of human responsibility, non-violence, and inter-religious understand-ing. He also stressed the fact that he was not seeking Tibetan independence but 'a meaningful autonomy' within the People's

Republic of China (PRC). He also mentioned the role that the United States could play in controlling the warming up of the planet and on fighting economic injustice.

From universal responsibility to initiations

The Dalai Lama's visits to countries outside India became a yearly occurrence, particularly to the United States in order to meet with the youth and to discuss science, mind, and religion, particularly at Emory University where he had been involved with American scientists. However, before the 2020 pandemic that is sweeping the world, he had already cut down on visits abroad because of medical advice. Some of the most important visits were related to invitations by leaders of religious traditions, and the emphasis since 2015 was on religious festivals, occasions for common prayer and meditation, and important moments for other religious traditions. The Dalai Lama explained on turning down many invitations that within his more limited availability he wanted to spend a significant amount of time leading initiations and performing Buddhist ceremonies. In doing so he emphasised non-violence and universal responsibility as central to the world of the 21st century.

As it was in 1989 when he received the Nobel Prize for Peace, the Dalai Lama made some occasions foundational for his ongoing world teaching on non-violence. In January 2012 he received the Mahatma Gandhi International Award for Reconciliation and Peace at Bodh Gaya, the place in which the Buddha Shakyamuni achieved enlightenment. In his acceptance speech, addressed to Mahatma Gandhi's granddaughter, he mentioned how sacred the place was for Buddhists.[10] Further, he recognised that Gandhi was an upholder of India's 3,000 years' tradition of *ahimsa*.[11] He explained that *ahimsa* means that whenever there is a problem one tries to solve it through dialogue and reconciliation. Gandhi carried such principle to the Indian independence struggle by carrying it through non-violence, a principle that was not accepted by all involved in the struggle against the British. In his speech the Dalai Lama considered himself a follower of the Mahatma and spoke again of the inner disarmament needed through inner peace to bring positive emotions and to avoid negative emotions in all actions. He reiterated that he was committed to non-violence for the rest of his life and that there was a task of disarmament for a peaceful world during the 21st century.[12]

Such message of non-violence was poignant because of the Dalai Lama's involvement in religious festivals of other traditions, particularly Hindu and Muslim festivals in India, breaking the foundations of ethnic and religious prejudice that go back to the Partition of India in 1947.[13] Thus, his appearance at the Kumbha Mela Hindu festival in India was welcome news within the Indian press in January 2013 when he visited Allahabad during the festival.[14] The Kumbha Mela festival offers the opportunity to millions of devotees to bathe in the river Ganges, the mother of all, and to achieve the fulfilment of *karma* and immortality. Besides the Ganges, there are two other sacred rivers located at Allahabad – the Yamuna and the Saraswathi. The Yamuna, like the Ganges, has its earthly origin in the Himalayas. The Saraswathi, however, is a mystical river, which has no physical form. It is believed that the Saraswathi exists only on the ethereal or spiritual plane and is invisible to the human eye. The Dalai Lama on attending the Kumbha Mela was honouring the historical connections between Buddhism and Hinduism and his support for such shared humanity. In 2010, and in connection with the Kumbha Mela, the Dalai Lama joined the activities of Parmarth Niketan, an ashram in Rishikesh where he joined yoga guru Swami Ramdev, NDA working chairman L.K. Advani, and others in the launching of the *Encyclopaedia of Hinduism*.[15]

One of the areas where non-violence and religious cooperation has been less forthcoming in the past few years has been the relations between the Dalai Lama and the Vatican. The Dalai Lama met Pope Benedict XVI in 2006; however, when he attended a meeting of Nobel Prize winners in Rome in December 2014 the Dalai Lama and Pope Francis did not meet.[16] While Pope Francis through the Vatican Press Office told the press that he held the Dalai Lama in very high regard a meeting did not take place as Pope Francis was trying to improve relations with China in order to safeguard the rights of Roman Catholics in China. As a result, Pope Francis did not meet any of the Nobel Prize winners who were meeting in Rome after South Africa had refused a visa to the Dalai Lama under pressure from China.[17]

With Muslims the Dalai Lama has kept an open dialogue and a sense of togetherness. Thus, for example, on his stay at the Ladakh region of the Jammu and Kashmir state of India in July 2016 he visited two mosques located beside a Buddhist monastery in the regional capital Leh.[18] Thus, after visiting the Jokhang Temple the Dalai Lama walked 50 metres to visit a Sunni mosque built in 1666–1667 by agreement of the Mughal Emperor Aurangzeb and the Ladakhi King Deltan Namgyal at that time. Prayers were held at the mosque with the participation of the Dalai Lama. Then, the Dalai Lama walked 200 metres to visit a Shia mosque where he met with the leader of the Shia community and some Shia clerics. Buddhists and Muslims joined in the Muslim prayers. The Shia leader reminded the participants that such visit was the third visit by the Dalai Lama to that mosque. The Dalai Lama recalled that during the era of the Fifth Dalai Lama, land was given to a group of Ladakhi Muslim traders to build a mosque marking the beginning of a Tibetan Muslim community in Tibet. Muslims in Tibet have taken part in all government activities and they are known as a very religious community 'characterised by their gentleness and peacefulness'. In several previous occasions the Dalai Lama, visiting Ladakh for the conferring of Buddhist initiation on large gatherings over summer, had been welcomed and hosted by the Muslim community.[19] Thus, on 16 July 2014 the Muslim Coordination Committee Leh had hosted a community reception for the Dalai Lama at the Grand Dragon Hotel.[20] On that occasion, the Dalai Lama spoke of his acquaintance with Muslims since childhood, and of his 'genuine admiration and respect for their religion'. He also thanked them for their good relations with Buddhists in Ladakh over time and the good relations within their own Muslim community. Further, as the Dalai Lama had done in his visits to the United States, he expressed his conviction that those terrorists who had conducted the attacks on the Twin Towers on 9/11 could not represent Islam as a faith. The Dalai Lama was clear in his messages regarding 9/11 that the terrorists were not 'Muslim terrorists' because no religion could adhere to terrorism, and that while the politicians and others needed to decide, his reading of any violent moment in humanity's history was towards the Mahatma's understanding that any violence would lead to more violence.[21]

The Dalai Lama's engagement with the Parliament of World Religions allowed him to meet diverse sectors of the religious communities and at the same time to continue fostering his shared humanity understanding of unity, inter-religious dialogue, and compassion.[22] The first Parliament of World Religions met in Chicago from 11–16 September 1893, and therefore the centenary meetings of 1993 became a catalyst for diverse meetings of all religions of the world. The meetings took place at the Palmer Hotel of Chicago and members of the different religions met to celebrate together and to see how they could address together some of the critical issues that challenged the world. Hans Küng's document 'Towards a Global Ethic: An Initial Declaration' set the agenda for the ten-day discussions. This kind of global ethic was taken as the agenda for the future and the Dalai Lama delivered the keynote speech on the last day of the meetings. In 1999 the Parliament met in Cape Town, South Africa, in 2004 in Barcelona in the Universal Forum of Cultures, in 2009 in Melbourne, Australia, in 2015 it took place at Salt Lake City, and in 2018 in Toronto. In 2015 the Parliament met at Salt Lake City and the Dalai Lama, together with Karen Armstrong, was once again one of the keynote speakers.[23]

In the following year, the Dalai Lama returned to Salt Lake City to meet with the Tibetan and Mormon community in Utah, as well as sharing lunch with Gary Herbert, Governor of Utah, and gave a talk to staff and students at the University of Utah.[24] It was his third visit to Utah with the first having taken place in 2001. On 22 June 2016, the Dalai Lama paid a courtesy call to the Three Counsellors of the Church of Jesus Christ of Latter-day Saints at their worldwide headquarters.[25] The visit took place on the occasion of the Dalai Lama's visit to the Utah Tibetan community at their newly established Tibetan Community Hall. He was greeted by Tashi Shölpa dancers, children carrying the 'Chema Changu', and the official greeting by the President of the Utah Tibetan Association Lobsang Tsering. Salt Lake County Mayor Ben McAdams was also present and spoke of the compassion by the Tibetan community that helped with the elderly, the homeless, and those in need. The Dalai Lama donated a painting of the seventeen masters of Nalanda representing the Tibetan contribution, as a peaceful and compassionate ancient civilisation, to the philosophical systems of the world. In explaining the Tibetan tradition of reason and logic, unique within Buddhism, the Dalai Lama brought the unique pride of Tibetan communities throughout the world. Especially important to his teachings was the mantra used for the consecration of objects: *Ye dharma hetuprabhava hetum tesham tathagata hyavadat tesham cha yo nirodha evam vadi mahashramana*

Of those things that arise from causes,
The Tathagata has taught those causes,
And also what their cessation is:
This is the doctrine of the Great Sage.

The Dalai Lama's visit to Utah included a ceremony for taking refuge and generating the awakening mind of *bodhichitta*. After he flew to Denver where he visited the Tibetan community there, he spoke to a large gathering at the University of Colorado.[26] It is to be noted that the Tibetan communities were very welcomed by the authorities of Utah and Colorado, and that the Tibetans had chosen not only urban centres in the United States but also places where snow is abundant throughout the winter, just like in Tibet.

In his outreach to Judaism the Dalai Lama has visited Israel several times with a mixed reception by the Israeli government due to pressure by China but always receiving a warm reception by Jewish religious leaders and Jews themselves. In 2006, for example, he paid his fourth visit to Israel and was asked difficult questions about his thoughts regarding China, the Palestinians, and the Israeli government. The Dalai Lama's honesty, compassion, and his peacekeeping and non-violence options were very clear. During that visit, the Israeli government did not have a meeting with him, and the Dalai Lama met with Palestinians activists. The Dalai Lama summarised the purpose of his visit as 'to promote human values and religious harmony' so that 'if we understand the value of other traditions, then we can develop mutual respect and mutual understanding'.[27] The Dalai Lama played down the impasse with the Israeli government saying that whenever he goes he doesn't want to create any inconvenience, and that the staff of the Chinese Embassy were only carrying out their duties set by the Chinese government. Regarding Hamas he suggested to wait to see what they do because they were elected democratically but he advised Hamas not to use violence as, according to the Dalai Lama, they will not achieve what they want. One of the main purposes of the Dalai Lama's visit in 2006 was to participate in the celebrations marking the birth centenary of Israel's first Prime Minister David Ben-Gurion who had a special interest in Buddhism.[28]

Europe remained the continent outside India where he paid more visits over the years, and Germany was the prime destination with thirty-seven visits between 1973 and 2014.[29] And within a series of visa rejections for the Dalai Lama because of pressure from the PRC it was the German government at federal level and at provincial level that always welcomed the Dalai Lama and his message.

However, his pilgrimages within India were occasions of deep communion with other traditions and of life as he visited places of significance for other traditions. One of his favourite visits has been to the Harmandir Sahib (the Golden Temple) in Amritsar, Punjab, again on 9 November 2019.[30] An older and more frail Dalai Lama spoke of Guru Nanak, the founder of Sikhism, summarising in my opinion his own life and journey as a peacemaker between religions, traditions, and peoples of the world. He said: 'Guru Nanak he himself took a pilgrimage to Mecca. That shows religious harmony. Also, imagine his followers, no caste system, that's a great thing. So, I whole heartedly admire Sikhism, no caste system. Then the "sardar ji", wherever they live they are hardworking'.[31]

The Dalai Lama has always stressed the connections between Buddhists, the Lord Buddha, and the foundations of Buddhist knowledge with Indian masters. Thus, he reminded others that Tibetans refer to India as 'our Aryabhoomi' (precious land).[32] The Dalai Lama's closeness to Indian thought and ancient Indian psychology and practices such as *Shamata* and *Vipassana* involve analytical meditation, and single minded-focus to analyse the nature of reality. Thus, Tibetan Buddhist knowledge comes from Indian Buddhist masters such as Najarjuna, Aryadeva, Buddhapalita, and Dharmakirti so that the Dalai Lama stated that 'all our knowledge comes from India'.[33] In that interview he also concluded that as different religions live in peace in India: 'I am completely convinced that religious harmony is possible everywhere'.[34]

Such spirit of peacekeeping was physically and spiritually expressed by the Dalai Lama in 2009 when in gratitude to the government of India and the people of India he prayed at eight different places of worship in New Delhi in communion with Hinduism and all other traditions, including the place of martyrdom of Mahatma Gandhi (Gandhi smriti), a Hindu temple, a mosque, a Sikh temple, a Christian church, a Jain temple, a Laxmi Narayan temple, and a Jewish synagogue.[35]

Conclusions: the Dalai Lama and universal responsibility

The figure of the Dalai Lama as a peacekeeper evolved throughout the life of a young Tibetan chosen as the 14th Dalai Lama and thereafter enthroned to lead Tibet as a political and spiritual leader. Throughout his education and Buddhist formation he learned values of compassion, interdependence, and non-violence. However, the unexpected happened as he had to leave Tibet for exile in India. As a result, he returned to the land of the Buddha's enlightenment and slowly was asked by those surrounding him to help them in their journey of self-discovery and politics. It was the awarding of the Nobel Prize for Peace in 1989 that made him into an international public figure. Thus, his own inner disarmament became a sign of the peacekeeper not only between Tibet and China, but in many occasions in which he aided peoples of nations throughout the world to control their minds and to foster and work for dialogue and peace. 'We are all human beings' became a mantra in his case and a realisation by those who listened to him. Thus, the Dalai Lama developed a message of compassion through interdependence with humans, animals, nature, and creation that quickly led to a shared and common global responsibility, and universal responsibility.

It was not by chance that during the global pandemic of COVID-19 in 2020 the Dalai Lama urged by 'The Call to Unite' wrote a declaration regarding the important issues within the pandemic.[36] He spoke of the threats to health and the sadness of those we have lost as well as the economic crisis and the impossibility of many to make a living through work. His message was clear: 'we must focus on what unites us as members of one family'. The Dalai Lama suggested to reach to each other with compassion because as human beings we are all the same. We share the same fears, hopes, uncertainties and we are all united by a desire for happiness. However, we share a great capacity to reason and to see reality to transform hardship into opportunity. Only by coming together globally, continues the Dalai Lama, we will be able to meet the 'unprecedented' challenges we face. Such declaration followed other public pronouncements the Dalai Lama had made since the start of the pandemic, including his Message for Earth Day.[37] In that message he reminded all that in a very difficult moment of a pandemic we are reminded of the value of compassion and mutual support, with a response as one humanity, providing for the essential needs of all. Within such message he reminded all that 'our mother earth is teaching us a lesson in universal responsibility'.

Indeed, the coronavirus pandemic provided the opportunity for the Dalai Lama to stress some of the messages of compassion and global responsibility that he had given to a global humanity for the past 40 years. In his words to *Time* magazine, in the context of a collection of testimonies on how the coronavirus has changed how we live our lives, he reiterated that the main weapon to fight the virus is compassion, and that he had no 'magical powers' as to solve the problem.[38] These words refer to the many requests he gets to solve some crisis while he knows physical suffering as anybody else in his old age so that 'we must also remember that nobody is free of suffering, and extend our hands to others who lack homes, resources or family to protect them'. He ended his testimony to *Time* magazine by stating that as a Buddhist he believes in the principle of impermanence, so that the virus will pass, and the global community will be rebuild once again.[39] These words expand on his initial declaration of 30 March 2020 in response to many requests in which he prays for an early end to the pandemic so that 'your peace and happiness may soon be restored'. His sound advice was to look after the vulnerable especially those 'with no stable income' whose life is a daily struggle. Further, his advice was to examine the problems in front of us by saying that 'if there is something to be done – do it, without any need to worry; if there is nothing to be done, worrying about it further will not help'.[40]

Notes

1   HH the 14th Dalai Lama, 'Universal Responsibility in the Modern World', Royal Albert Hall, London, 22 May 2008 in Subhash C. Kashyap, *The Political Philosophy of the Dalai Lama: Selected Speeches and Writings*. New Delhi: Rupa Publications, 2014, pp. 446–458 at p. 447.

2   http://www.dalailama.emory.edu/about/professor.html Accessed 8 May 2020.

3   https://compassion.emory.edu/ Accessed 8 May 2020.

4   http://www.dalailama.emory.edu/about/ETSI.html Accessed 8 May 2020.

5   Alex Klugerman, 'Dalai Lama Delays Emory Visit', *The Emory Wheel* 25 August 2017.

6   'Profs, Dalai Lama Compare Religious, Secular Ethics', *The Emory Wheel* 10 October 2013.

7   The Dalai Lama, *Beyond Religion: Ethics for a Whole World*. Boston, MA: Houghton, Mifflin, and Harcourt, 2011.

8   The 2013 program of the Dalai Lama's visit is available at http://www.dalailama.emory.edu/Visit%202013%20Program.pdf Accessed 8 May 2020.

9   https://www.dalailama.com/messages/acceptance-speeches/u-s-congressional-gold-medal/congressional-gold-medal Accessed 8 May 2020.

10 HH the 14th Dalai Lama, 'Commitment to Non-Violence: Mahatma Gandhi International Award for Reconciliation and Peace', Bodh Gaya, 4 January 2012 in Kashyap, *The Political Philosophy of the Dalai Lama*, pp. 559–560.

11 Kashyap, *The Political Philosophy of the Dalai Lama*, p. 559.

12 Kashyap, *The Political Philosophy of the Dalai Lama*, p. 560.

13 Mario I. Aguilar, *Interreligious Dialogue and the Partition of India: Hindus and Muslims in Dialogue about Violence and Forced Migration*. London: Jessica Kingsley, 2018.

14 'Dalai Lama Likely to Attend Kumbh Mela at Allahabad', *NDTV* 7 January 2013 at https://www.ndtv.com/allahabad-news/dalai-lama-likely-to-attend-kumbh-mela-at-allahabad-509639

15 Central Tibetan Administration, 'His Holiness the Dalai Lama Participates in Maha Kumbh Mela', 6 April 2010 at https://tibet.net/his-holiness-the-dalai-lama-participates-in-maha-kumbh-mela/

16 'Pope Benedict XVI Meets with Dalai Lama', *Fox News* 13 January 2015 at https://www.foxnews.com/story/pope-benedict-xvi-meets-with-dalai-lama

17 'Pope Declines Dalai Lama Meeting in Rome', *BBC News* 12 December 2014 at https://www.bbc.com/news/world-europe-30455187

18 'Dalai Lama Visits Shia and Sunni Mosques in Ladakh, Jammu & Kashmir', *Tibetan Review* 30 July 2016 at https://www.tibetanreview.net/dalai-lama-visits-shia-and-sunni-mosques-in-ladakh-jammu-kashmir/ Accessed 8 May 2020.

19 In July 2014 (3–12) the Dalai Lama was in Ladakh to confer the Kalachakra empowerment, an event attended by 150,000 people from 60 different countries.

20 'Ladakh Muslims Host Reception for Dalai Lama', *Tibetan Review* 18 July 2014 at https://www.tibetanreview.net/ladakh-muslims-host-reception-for-dalai-lama/ Accessed 8 May 2020.

21 'Relevant Comments by HH the Dalai Lama Subsequent to the Sept. 11, 2001 Terrorist Attack on the US' at https://www.dalailama.com/messages/world-peace/9-11 Accessed 8 May 2020.

22 https://parliamentofreligions.org/ Accessed 8 May 2020.

23 'Dalai Lama to Address 2015 Parliament of World Religions', *Tibetan Review* 7 December 2014 at https://www.tibetanreview.net/dalai-lama-to-address-2015-parliament-of-worlds-religions/ Accessed 8 May 2020.

24 'Dalai Lama Visits Utah, Talks about China, Compassion and Humanity', *The Indian Express* 22 June 2016 Accessed 9 May 2020.

25 https://www.dalailama.com/news/2016/his-holiness-the-dalai-lama-visits-utah-tibetan-association Accessed 9 May 2020.

26 'Dalai Lama Addressed Capacity Crowd of 9000 in University of Colorado', *Tibetan Review* 28 June 2016 at https://www.tibetanreview.net/dalai-lama-addressed-capacity-crowd-of-9000-in-university-of-colorado/ Accessed 9 May 2020.

27 Jay Michaelson, 'In Search of Religious Rationality, Dalai Lama Visits … the Mideast', *Forward* 24 February 2006 at https://forward.com/news/1101/in-search-of-religious-rationality-dalai-lama-vis/ Accessed 9 May 2020.

28 'The Dalai Lama to Visit Israel in February', *Hindustan Times* 23 January 2006 at https://www.hindustantimes.com/india/the-dalai-lama-to-visit-israel-in-february/story-YDRoniaTtvbDAkek1Wj7yM.html Accessed 9 May 2020.

29 'Dalai Lama Concludes Fruitful Visit to Frankfurt', *Tibetan Review* 21 May 2014 at https://www.tibetanreview.net/dalai-lama-concludes-fruitful-visit-to-frankfurt-2/ Accessed 8 May 2020.

30 https://www.sikhnet.com/news/dalai-lama-i-wholeheartedly-admire-sikhism See video at https://www.youtube.com/watch?list=RDCMUCiPJ_g02LuOgOG0ZNk5j1jA&v=U2LWDyfRk70&-feature=emb_rel_end Accessed 9 May 2020.

31 https://www.sikhnet.com/news/dalai-lama-i-wholeheartedly-admire-sikhism Accessed 9 May 2020.

32 Vidya Venkat, 'India Is Our Aryabhoomi: Dalai Lama', *The Hindu* 16 June 2018 at https://www.thehindu.com/society/india-is-our-aryabhoomi-dalai-lama/article24180001.ece Accessed 9 May 2020.

33 Vidya Venkat, 'India Is Our Aryabhoomi: Dalai Lama', *The Hindu* 16 June 2018.

34 Vidya Venkat, 'India Is Our Aryabhoomi: Dalai Lama', *The Hindu* 16 June 2018.

35 See https://www.youtube.com/watch?v=iZ83IoLxUL8 Accessed 9 May 2020.

36 'His Holiness the Dalai Lama: World Should Unite for a Coordinated Global Response to COVID-19', 3 May 2020 at https://www.dalai-lama.com/news/2020/message-from-his-holiness-the-dalai-lama

37 'His Holiness the Dalai Lama's Message for Earth Day', Message requested by Global Water 2020, 22 April 2020 at https://www.dalailama.com/news/2020/his-holiness-the-dalai-lamas-message-for-earth-day

38 '"Prayer is Not Enough": The Dalai Lama on Why We Need to Fight Coronavirus with Compassion', 14 April 2020 at https://www.dalailama.com/news/2020/prayer-is-not-enough-the-dalai-lama-on-why-we-need-to-fight-coronavirus-with-compassion

39 '"Prayer is Not Enough": The Dalai Lama on Why We Need to Fight Coronavirus with Compassion', *Time* 24 April 2020 at https://time.com/5820613/dalai-lama-coronavirus-compassion/

40 'A Special Message from His Holiness the Dalai Lama', 30 March 2020 at https://www.dalailama.com/news/2020/a-special-message-from-his-holiness-the-dalai-lama

INDEX

Printed in Great Britain
by Amazon

31232569R00059